When FOOTBALL *Was* FOOTBALL

FULHAM

First published in 2011

A catalogue record for this book is available from the British Library

ISBN: 978-0-857330-49-9

Published by Haynes Publishing, Sparkford, Yeovil,
Somerset BA22 7JJ, UK
Tel: 01963 442030 Fax: 01963 440001
Int. tel: +44 1963 442030 Int. fax: +44 1963 440001
E-mail: sales@haynes.co.uk
Website: www.haynes.co.uk

Haynes North America Inc., 861 Lawrence Drive,
Newbury Park, California 91320, USA

Creative Director: Kevin Gardner
Designed for Haynes by BrainWave

Printed and bound in the US

When
FOOTBALL *Was* FOOTBALL

FULHAM

A Nostalgic Look at a Century of the Club

Richard Allen

Contents

Introduction

Craven Cottage, home of Fulham Football Club. To watch a game from the river side of the ground is to see a scene that has barely changed since 1908, or even since 1932 or 1948. The Stevenage Road Stand – now named for Johnny Haynes, Fulham's greatest player – looks just as it always has: rows and rows of spectators, divided horizontally by a wall halfway up and vertically by view-restricting pillars, and most of all the windows at the back of the stand, in front of which those mysterious dark silhouetted heads watch the action. They could be anyone, from any time. Above this is a grey slate roof, a proud central gable, and the words "Fulham Football Club" painted in black on white. This is home. "Craven Cottage, by the river, take me home."

Early Days
1879-1945

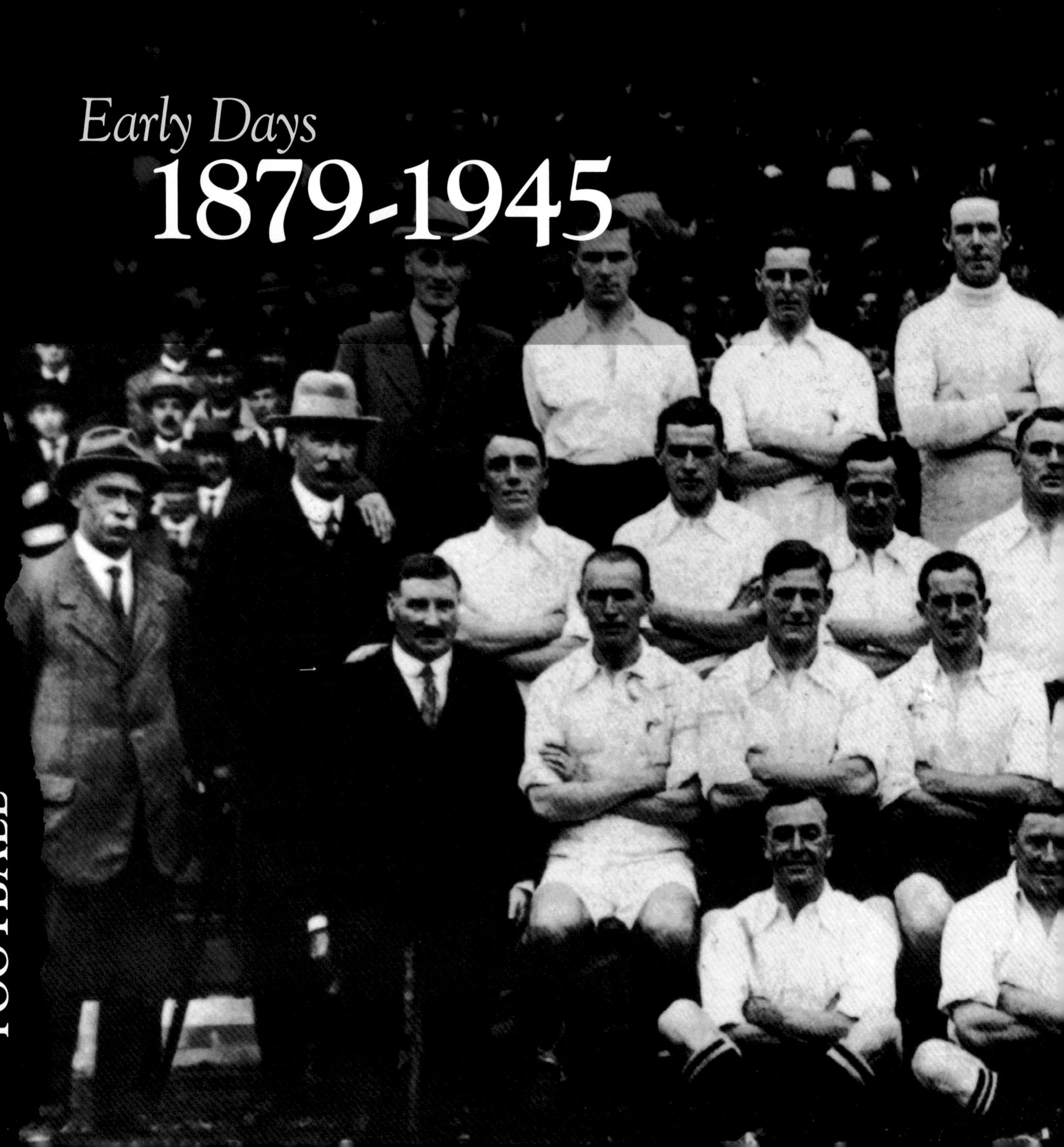

Where it all began. Highlights from this era include election to the Football League for the 1907–08 season and winning Division Three South in 1931–32.

Fulham FC, 1920.

The Founding of the Football Club

The club we now know as Fulham FC was formed in 1879 by the Revd Cardwell of St Andrew's Church, Fulham, and the Revd Propert of St Augustine's Mission, Lillie Road. Tom Norman, just 15 years old, was the club's first secretary, and its first established kit was light and dark blue quartered jerseys.

The team – known as Fulham St Andrew's – played at the Mud Pond, Star Road, Fulham, just over a mile away from the current stadium. Soon the club moved to Ranelagh Gardens, near Putney Bridge (the Eight Bells, now often an away fans' pub, was used for changing rooms), then spent time at various locations around Barnes and Putney.

In 1889 the name Fulham Football Club was adopted. Five years later, in 1894, a derelict site upriver became available, and while it took two years to get it ready for the game, it represented a permanent base from which the club might continue to grow. Fulham had found Craven Cottage.

The team changed its colours, this time to red shirts with white sleeves. On 10th October 1896 Fulham won their first game at Craven Cottage, a 4-0 win over Minerva in a Middlesex Senior Cup tie.

With a new ground Fulham won the Southern League Division Two title in 1901–02, won it again in 1902–03, and joined the Southern League Division One in 1903–04. Archibald Leitch's Craven Cottage was completed in 1905, and Fulham played Portsmouth before 20,000 people in the new ground's first game (a 0-0 draw).

1905–06 *Southern League Winners*

By 4 goals to 1 West Ham defeated Fulham on the latter's ground on Saturday. (1) Jarvis scoring a penalty goal for West Ham. (2) Fulham half-back with the ball. (3, 4, and 5) Studies of Fryer, the Fulham goalkeeper, saving hot shots.—(*Daily Mirror* photographs

HUGE CROWD AT CRAVEN COTTAGE.

After the enclosure was filled with a crowd of 25,000 people the Putney Bridge gate gave way, and two or three thousand people rushed in.

At Craven Cottage on Saturday Fulham defeated Plymouth Argyle by 2 to 0.—(*Daily Mirror* photograph.)

Having won the 1905–06 Southern League Division One title Fulham decided to aim higher. "Fulham have taken the plunge and have applied for admission to the Second League," read the *Daily Mirror*. Despite reports that Chelsea were opposing the application (a simple case of tit for tat: Fulham had successfully – with Tottenham – opposed Chelsea's application for the Southern League in 1905), Fulham were confident of success. With their excellent facilities and proven team, they were a club on the up.

Fulham's application faced bids from Bradford United, Burton Town, Chesterfield Town, Lincoln City, Oldham Athletic, Rotherham Town, Salford United and Wigan Town. In the event Fulham took 28 votes, Lincoln 23, Chesterfield 23, Oldham 17, Bradford 11, Burton 7, and the others none. Fulham resigned its first team from the Southern League at the league's dinner at Holborn. Fulham's first ever Football League game was at home to Hull City. The line-up was: Skene, Ross, Lindsay, Collins, Morrison, Goldie, Dalrymple, Freeman, Bevan, Hubbard and Threlfall. Fulham lost 1-0, a defeat described both as disastrous and wretched. But after that they beat newly relegated Derby 1-0 (Walter Freeman scored the milestone goal), then thrashed Lincoln City 6-1 at the Cottage, a win which is said to have reassured supporters.

41,000 PEOPLE WATCH FULHAM BEAT MANCHESTER UNITED

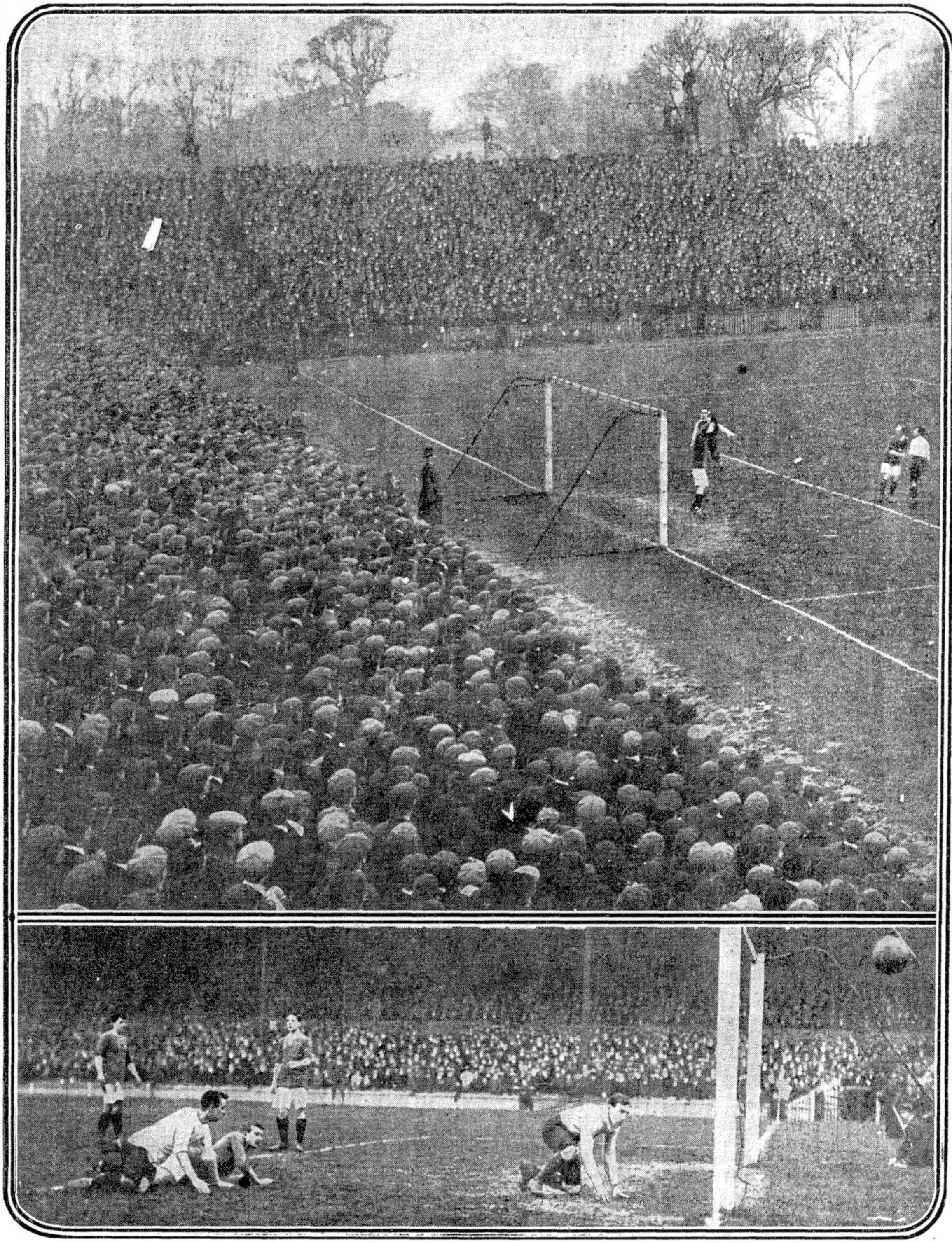

The great feature of Saturday afternoon's English Cup-tie matches was the game at the Craven Cottage ground, where Fulham beat Manchester United by 2 goals to 1, thus qualifying for the semi-final round. The victory surprised and delighted the thousands of Southerners present, and the most intense enthusiasm prevailed.

The upper picture, which shows a portion of the vast crowd, was taken at the moment when Moger made a brilliant save for Manchester. In the lower photograph Skene, the Fulham goalkeeper (near the posts) is watching the ball going into the net. This was Manchester's only goal. —(*Daily Mirror* and Half-Tones.)

December 1908: A huge crowd of 35,000 watch Fulham lose 3-2 at home to Tottenham. According to the *Daily Mirror*, "Enormous interest centred round the battle between North and West London."

The wins began to pile up, and in the New Year Fulham went to Luton in the FA Cup and won 8-3. In the next round they faced Norwich, who had beaten the holders Sheffield Wednesday in the First Round. The *Daily Mirror* expected a Fulham win, though, calling Fulham "at their best, nearly as good a side as can be found in the country". Sure enough, Fulham won 2-1.

After a 1-1 draw at Manchester City in the Third Round, Fulham won a hard-fought replay 3-1. City led at the half after a goal from a free-kick, awarded after Harry Ross, the Fulham right-back, almost took a City player's head off with a tackle. There was a suggestion that the tackle had been a retaliation against an earlier off the ball incident, when Fulham's Threlfall had been tackled from behind by Jackson, City's left-back, with the ball more than 10 yards away.

Fulham won a penalty in the second half when City's Kelso handled the ball on the goal-line. Harry Ross took the penalty, but fired it too near the goalkeeper. Luckily for Ross the ball came straight back to him, and he drove home the equalizer. Fred Harrison then made it 2-1 to Fulham, finding time in the middle of a crowded area to slot home. Fireworks were let off in the crowd. The bad-tempered game flared up further when Harrison was badly fouled by Buchan of City, but justice was done when Dalrymple made it 3-1, thereby settling the tie.

Fulham had dominated all aspects of the game against their more illustrious opponents. A crowd of 37,000 watched; a huge number for the time.

In the next round, the quarter-final, Fulham drew Manchester United. This was an even harder game: United went on to win the First Division quite comfortably that season, but again Fulham rose to the occasion. Harrison converted a Goldie header to make it 1-0, United came back with a Sandy Turnbull strike, but Harrison scored again in the second half with a shot from long range.

The semi-final against Newcastle, played at Anfield, in Liverpool, was a rout. Fulham lost 6-0, although Skene in the Fulham goal was badly injured by a rough challenge from Newcastle's Appleyard, which meant he couldn't get to a number of shots that he might ordinarily have dealt with. Nevertheless, the game wasn't close, which was a huge disappointment after the previous rounds' heroics.

The 1921–22 season looked like being one of the club's more successful campaigns. Centre-forward Barney Travers, bought from Sunderland in February 1921, had been a frequent goal-scorer, but in March 1922 he was accused of bribery during an away trip in South Shields. He was tried, found guilty, and banned for life; Fulham's season then petered out (five of the last six games were lost).

The Whites spent much of the early 1920s in the top half of the Second Division, and much of the late 1920s in the bottom half.

In 1925–26 Fulham enjoyed a fine run in the FA Cup, beating Everton, Liverpool and Notts County before being stopped by Manchester United in the last eight.

In 1927–28 they were relegated into Division Three South.

1931–32 *Division Three South Champions*

In 1931–32 Fulham won Division Three South, scoring 111 goals along the way. Jim Hammond, who played cricket for Sussex at the time, scored 33 of them, including four in a 10-2 win over Torquay in September.

Frank Newton was another important player for the Whites. Newton had been signed from Stockport County in the pre-season. He'd scored 120 goals in three seasons for Stockport, and had agreed to join Ashton National for the 1931 season. Fulham interjected and Newton went on to score 81 in 88 games for the club. He was then sold to Reading for what manager James McIntyre called "a very substantial fee," but which may only have been £650.

The deal was a surprise to everyone. Fulham had rejected numerous offers for Newton already, and Reading were a Third Division club. Next season McIntyre signed Jack Lambert from Arsenal for £2,500, which didn't work out, and it is thought that the two incidents may have contributed to McIntyre being dismissed in February 1934, when the team were going well in Division Two. Mr Dudley Evans, a Fulham director, noted the club and McIntyre no longer saw eye to eye on tactics, and so "we did not feel disposed to retain a manager who was not in agreement on all points. At the same time we have parted good friends." He continued, slightly curiously: "It is just as if Mr McIntyre had died suddenly."

RIGHT: Fulham lose 3-0 to Watford in the FA Cup Third Round replay.

Play near the Chesterfield goal-mouth during the match against Fulham at Craven Cottage last night. The result was a draw, 2 all.

FRAYED TEMPERS AT FULHAM

Cottagers Fail to Take Their Chances Against Chesterfield

BY THE SPHINX

Frayed tempers marred the closing stages of the match at Craven Cottage, where Fulham and Chesterfield drew with two goals each.

With a greasy ball and slippery ground in the second half, classic football could hardly be expected, but Chesterfield resorted to rather rough tactics, which could not be condoned.

Fulham started so well that it looked as if they would run up a big score. Within five minutes Finch put them ahead. He took a well-placed pass in his stride, tricked Wass and fired the ball into the far corner.

It came as a surprise when Chesterfield broke away and scored after twenty minutes. Abel took a pass from the left and lobbed over Iceton's head.

VISITORS IMPROVE

The visitors improved now, but Fulham took the lead again, Gibbons scoring from a penalty when Hammond was tripped.

Shortly before half-time the scores were again level, when Abel scored from Austin's centre with a splendid header.

Fulham should have had a useful lead at this point, but weak finishing and a rather unsound defence allowed Chesterfield to keep on terms.

In the second half the football was of the kick and miss variety. Fulham had most of the play and plenty of chances, which they could not take.

The Cottagers have not much to worry about. Possibly their defence could be strengthened and their shooting must improve.

In March 1932 a 0-0 draw with bottom of the league Thames FC is worthy of a brief digression. Thames played in the league between 1930 and 1932. They were formed to play in the 120,000-seat West Ham Stadium at Custom House, London, a giant oval that was also used for speedway racing. Impressive enough, but nobody came to watch, and this, combined with some genuinely awful results, prompted Thames to not apply for re-election after finishing bottom of the table in 1931–32. That Fulham should draw 0-0 with such a team (and be lucky to do so) is entirely Fulhamish, as is the 8-0 win over the same opposition that followed at Craven Cottage three days later.

Fulham fought well in what was a very competitive division, and deserved their success. Reading, Southend, Crystal Palace and Brentford all had good spells, and all finished with more than 50 points, but Fulham's final tally of 57 was just enough.

Historical curiosity: in October it was reported that the club had made an annual loss of £4,340 from gate receipts of £17,695.

Fulham nearly did it again in 1932–33, finishing third in Division Two. Frank Newton was once more the star, scoring 27 in 31 games.

The team had started the season brightly but faltered in the New Year. Three straight defeats to open 1933 were followed by a win over Port Vale, then two draws. It amounted to one win in six, at which point McIntyre announced the signing of Mike Keeping and John Arnold from Southampton. The Fulham Chairman called the deal "a stroke of genius."

With the new signings aboard Fulham lost only one of their next 12 games, but unsurprisingly couldn't maintain that sort of form for the rest of the season. There was no shame in finishing behind Stoke and Spurs, two good teams, but opportunities had been missed. Fulham took nothing from two games against struggling Grimsby, one point from relegated Chesterfield, and also lost 3-0 to Lincoln while in top form.

Early in 1933–34 Newton was sold, replaced by Jack Lambert at great cost. Newton had been prolific throughout his Fulham career; Lambert managed four in his 34 Fulham appearances. McIntyre was dismissed, and never worked in football again.

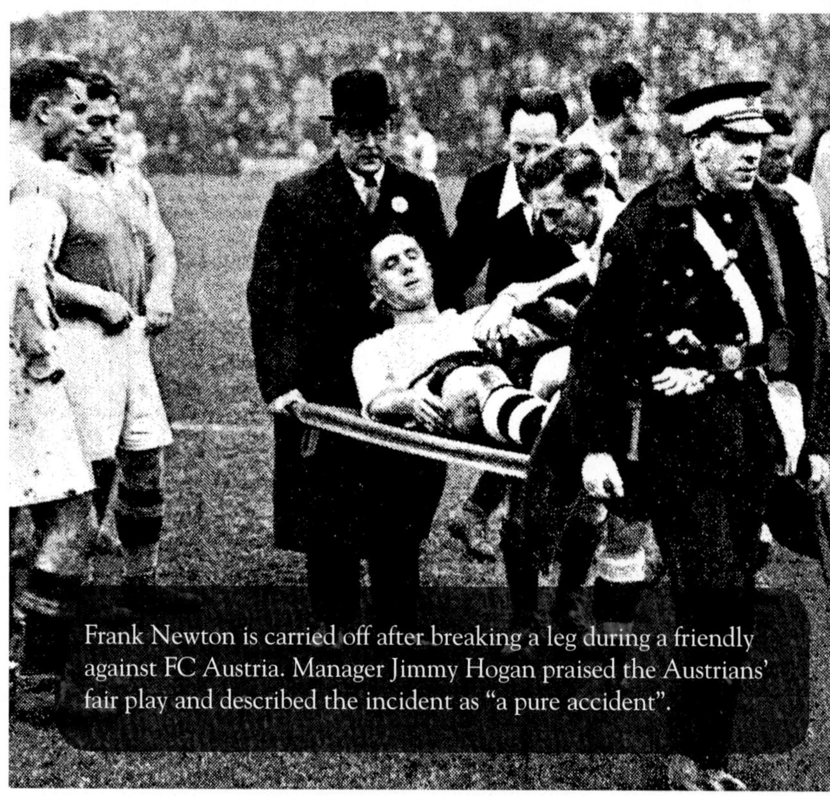

Frank Newton is carried off after breaking a leg during a friendly against FC Austria. Manager Jimmy Hogan praised the Austrians' fair play and described the incident as "a pure accident".

Page 30 THE DAILY MIRROR Wednesday, November 7, 1934

'YOU TRAITOR' TAUNT TO MANAGER HOGAN

Gibe About Giving the Italian Side a Few Wrinkles—and His Reply

WHAT WE MUST DO TO WIN

By JAMES HOGAN, the Famous Fulham and Continental Coach

"Hogan, you traitor!"

Not pleasant wo.ds these to have hurled at you—as they were at me in the Austria v. Scotland match at Hampden Park last year, when I went to the assistance of injured Austrian players under my care.

On that occasion the criticism came from the popular side of the ground.

A few weeks ago a prominent gentleman in English football remarked, "I suppose you will be going into the Italian dressing room to give the players a few wrinkles about English football and tactics."

My response was, "No, sir! But I should dearly love to be allowed into our dressing room to have a 'heart-to-heart' talk with the English international side about Italian football, which I have known since 1912."

Surely our people must know that we British football coaches have gone abroad to teach the foreigner because it has been a case of (1) not wanted at home, or (2) the Continental clubs have offered us much better terms.

Commendatore Pozzo

There are at least half a dozen intelligent ex-English international players abroad at present who are eating their hearts out to get home, but it appears to be a case of "not wanted."

I am hitting straight from the shoulder when I state that some poor mortals at home read their newspaper and are firmly convinced of the fact that it was a case of a tired team, bad "ref," hard ground, long journey, etc., but we British coaches—who were eye-witnesses of these games—know otherwise.

Every single member of the English international touring side admitted that our eleven was defeated last spring at Budapest and Prague by teams which played better football than we did.

ITALY HAS STUDIED US

Italy won the so-called football championship of the world last spring, and fully intend to beat us.

They have studied our style of play. The team is in special training. They have played together many times

The man at the helm, Vittorio Pozzo (Hugo Meisl the Second) knows our game from A to Z. The men are absolutely fired with patriotism, and ground conditions will not affect them in the least.

They will have a tremendous following and Italians will take London by storm. I know them and admire their enthusiasm.

The question now to be answered is: Can we beat the world's football champions? I reply: Yes! But we shall have to play much better than we did in the inter-League against Scotland.

The position at present is one-all between the two countries. We played a draw against Italy on their own ground at the end of our season and under favourable conditions for the Italians.

We think and hope that our friends will not make excuses now that they must measure swords with us under our conditions. If we adopt the following methods I am of the opinion that England will win:—

1. Our players must be inspired by patriotism, and realise that they are to uphold the prestige of British football.
2. We must concentrate and fight for the whole of the ninety minutes, even if we have a three-goals lead. There must be no quarter, as we have a great deal to win back.
3. We must play intelligent football, keep the ball on the ground as much as possible, and be constructive with every pass. Every movement an object—the Italian goal.
4. We must concentrate more on attack than defence.
5. There must be no aimless kicking but more placing of the ball.
6. We must draw the opponents, pass the ball and run into position.
7. Every English player must work overtime, fight for every ball and harass the opposition as much as possible.

If we play the game as it should be played my tip is four to one for England.

ITALY MATCH BRIEFS

"England has not had such a team for years and Italy has a hard nut to crack," is the opinion of next Wednesday's big match given yesterday to Reuter by Herr Meisl, Austrian football dictator.

* * *

Mr. H. J. Huband, F.A. member in charge of the England team, said yesterday that our players would go to a quiet spot in Hertfordshire to talk over tactics before the match. But there will be no special training.

* * *

Italy's final trial matches were played in Turin yesterday and fifteen players selected to make the trip.

* * *

Mr. James Hogan, famous manager and Continental coach, will criticise the match exclusively in the "Daily Mirror." Coming from one whose knowledge of European football is unrivalled, his views will be of exceptional interest. This will be in addition to Adjutant's report of the match.

Jimmy Hogan took charge in May 1934. Hogan's career was unconventional, his methods never entirely trusted by the conservative British footballing community, but his influence was extraordinary. The great Hungarian side of 1953? They acknowledged that Hogan had taught them everything they knew. Austria's 1930s Wunderteam? Hogan had a hand in that too. He also strongly influenced Béla Guttmann, the Hungarian coach credited with bringing 4-2-4 to Brazil, the formation that underpinned that country's dominance from the 1950s to the 1970s.

So Hogan was quite the pickup. He cleverly signed Frank Newton back from Reading, and introduced himself to Fulham in the club's 1934–35 yearbook as follows: "After spending a score of years in exile, teaching the foreigner how to play, I now make my bow as manager-coach to my dear old club. Can you imagine how honoured and delighted I feel?"

Training in England at the time was largely fitness-based, with a genuine belief that players starved of a ball during the week will want it more during matches. Hogan took the opposite view, and taught the possession game and individual skills, which itself caused problems as it exposed some of the players' limitations and made them uncomfortable. His methods were far ahead of their time and the players simply didn't adapt.

There was a suggestion that Fulham were trying too hard to do too much. The following, written after a 2-1 defeat to West Ham, was typical:

"Did they [West Ham] deserve it? Most emphatically they did! Did they play football on anything like the classic lines of the Cottagers? Most emphatically they did not. But it is possible to have too much of a good thing and in this match Fulham seemed obsessed with the idea that if a thing was worth doing at all it was worth doing properly. In fact, if they could not get goals by the Hogan plan they disdained to get them at all. West Ham were content to get them 'any old how'."

As, it must be said, was this: "Fulham are producing the type of football that makes the turnstiles sing."

It is thought that the players lost confidence and after 31 games, while Hogan was in hospital with appendicitis, Fulham sacked him. His contract was to expire on 1st June, and Fulham's board declared that he was not expected to be back that season. Or at all, as it transpired: Fulham sent a director to the hospital and confirmed the decision to end his contract. Hogan took legal action and was found in the right, but he was more disappointed that his attempts to prove himself in England had ended so badly.

The Fulham team clear snow from the pitch before an FA Cup match against Bury, January 1939. The match finished 6-0 to Fulham, and Ronnie Rooke scored all the goals. Before the game Rooke had told a friend “I don’t know what’s wrong with me. My shots always seem to be going the wrong way.” Clearly something clicked, and Rooke walked off with the match ball and a new club record for goals in a single game.

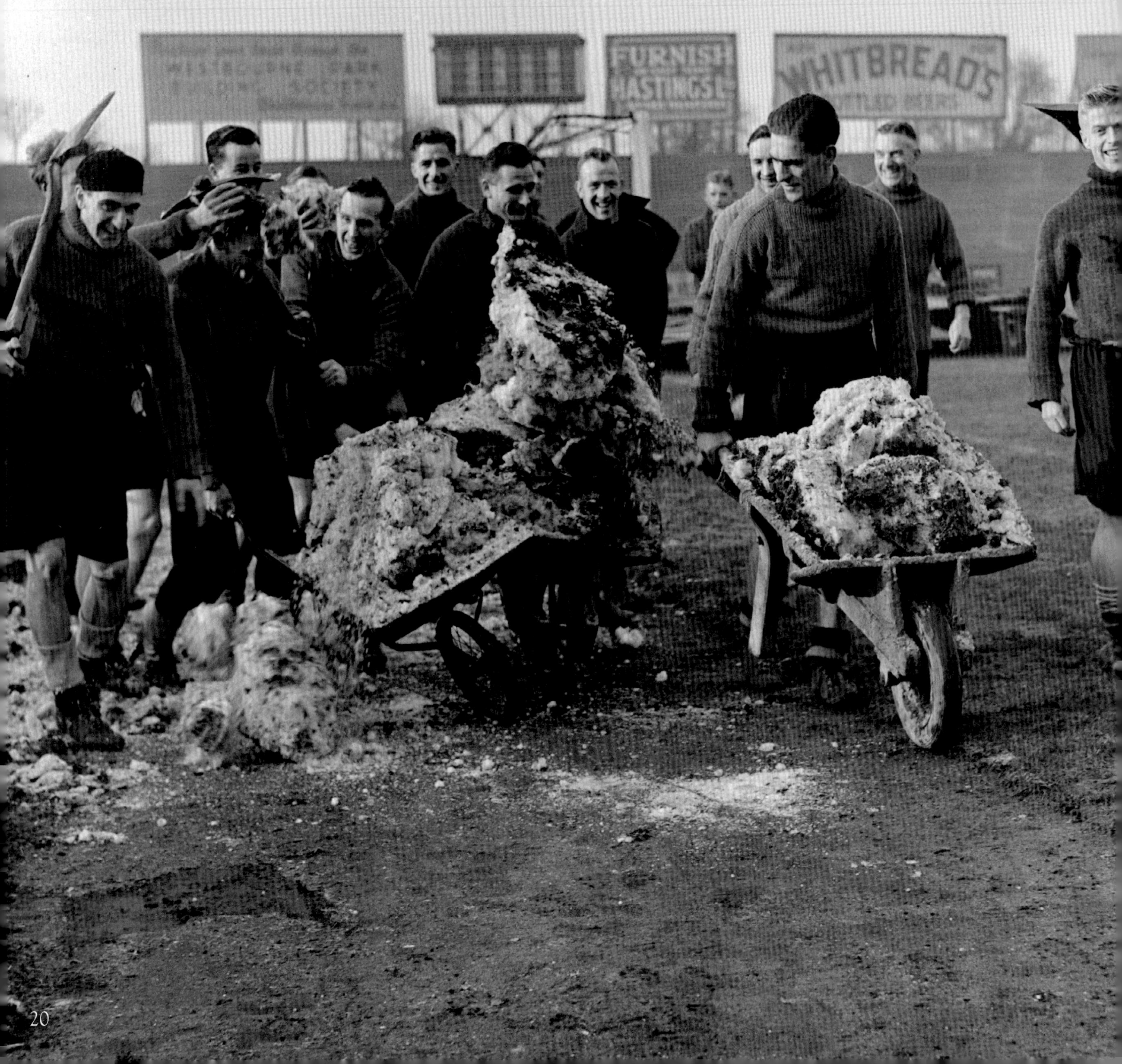

–LEGENDS–

Ronnie Rooke

Ronnie Rooke's best days were interrupted by the Second World War, but despite this he managed to put together a phenomenal career.

Crystal Palace bought Rooke from Woking in 1933, but with their existing centre-forward, Peter Simpson, so productive (Simpson scored 153 in 180 games in his Palace career), Rooke didn't get a look in.

Fulham took note. They liked his strength and the power of his shooting, but mostly they liked his goals: Rooke had scored 160 in three seasons of Palace reserve team football. In 1936 a deal was struck, and for £300 Fulham had a new centre-forward.

It was an inspired signing. Before the outbreak of war Rooke scored 63 times in 90 games. *During* the war he was unstoppable, blasting another 212 in 199 games (including a ridiculous 27 in 15 in 1944–45). He played parts of two more seasons after the war, then surprisingly left for Arsenal in 1946. There he scored another 68 goals in 88 games.

RIGHT: Ronnie Rooke in August 1938.

FOOTBALL
–STATS–

Ronnie Rooke

Name: Ronnie Rooke

Born: Guildford 1912

Died: Bedford 1985

Position: Centre-forward

Fulham playing career: 1936–1947 (includes gap for the Second World War)

Club appearances: 110 (does not include wartime football)

Goals: 78 (does not include wartime football)

Craven Cottage, Boxing Day 1945. Fulham won 5-2, Rooke scored four goals. The teams had also played one another on Christmas Day in what was then a familiar feature of the fixture list. In the photo Fulham's Dennis Rampling challenges Portsmouth's Harry Walker. Rampling scored five goals in 15 games that season, his best haul ever.

RIGHT: The crowd of 22,324 enjoys Fulham's win.

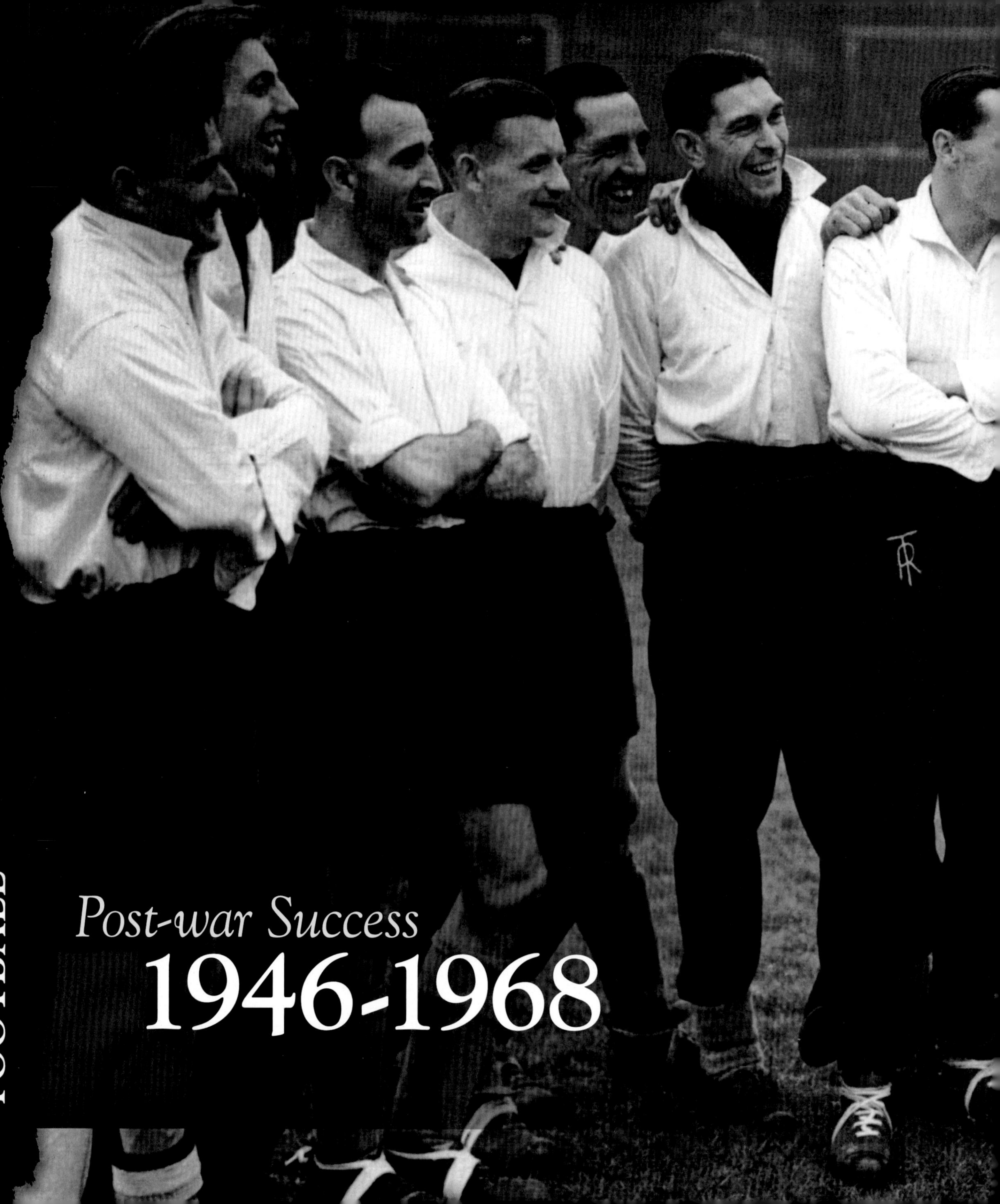

Post-war Success
1946-1968

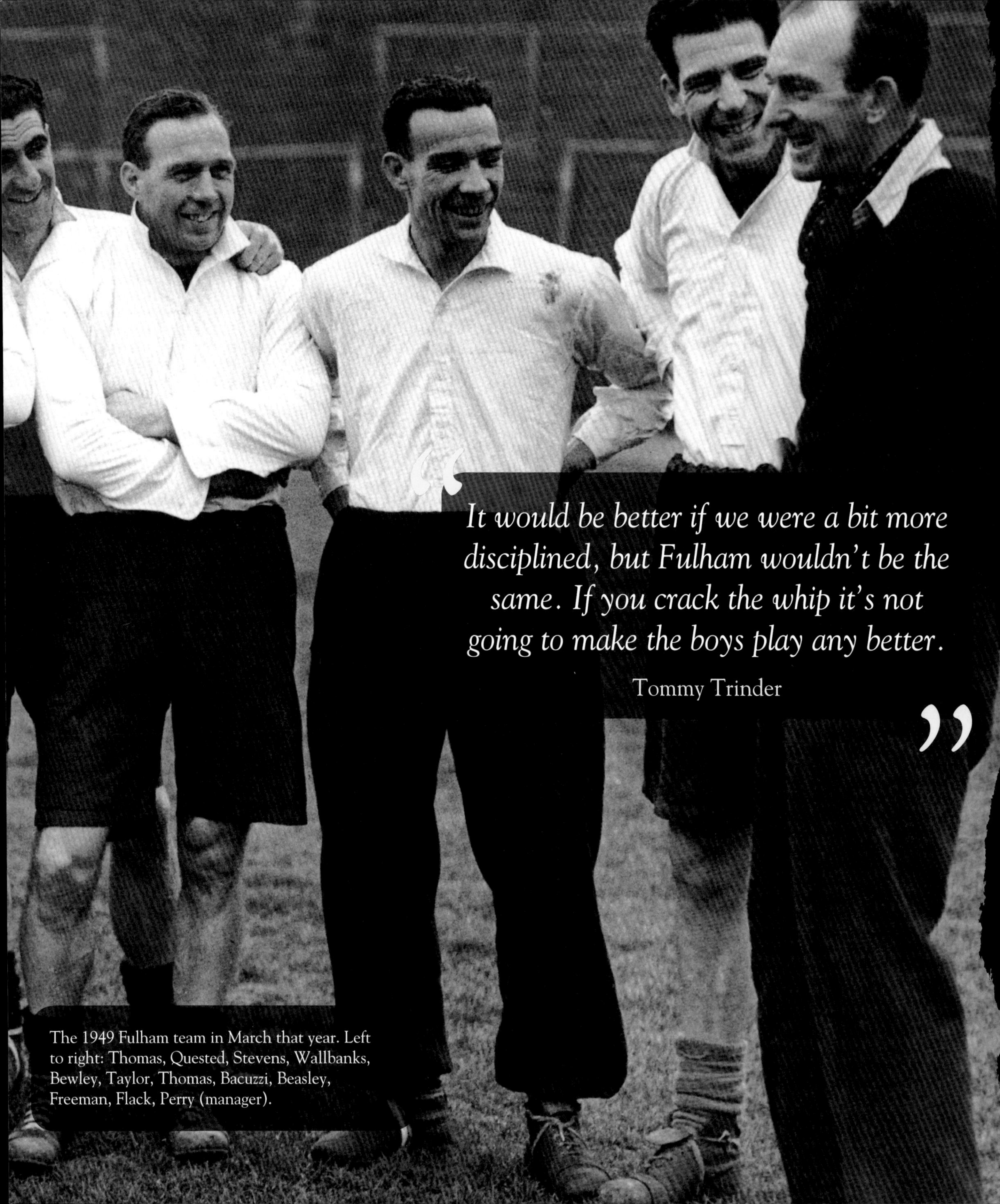

It would be better if we were a bit more disciplined, but Fulham wouldn't be the same. If you crack the whip it's not going to make the boys play any better.

Tommy Trinder

The 1949 Fulham team in March that year. Left to right: Thomas, Quested, Stevens, Wallbanks, Bewley, Taylor, Thomas, Bacuzzi, Beasley, Freeman, Flack, Perry (manager).

Fulham emerged from the war with two unremarkable mid-table seasons, but in 1948–49 won Division Two by a point from West Bromwich Albion.

Fulham won only three of their first 10 games, but a spurt in October kick-started the season. After a 5-0 thrashing of QPR (Bob Thomas two, Arthur Stevens three), the team won five of their next seven. None of these games were decided by more than a single goal, suggesting to some that Fulham were playing above themselves.

But in December Fulham signed Arthur Rowley from West Bromwich and blazed their way through the rest of the season. Rowley bagged 19 in 22 from the centre-forward position, a triumph for player and club, for Fulham had shrewdly brought Rowley inside from the wing, where he hadn't been a success at WBA. It was a switch that changed his career.

While his brother, Jack, was more famous (he played for Manchester United and England), it was Arthur who left his name in the game's record books. Nobody before or since has scored more league goals in their career: Rowley's 434 in 619 games is some way ahead of his

April 2, 1949

k Osborne uses
am's loudspeaker
m to instruct
rs in a practice
at Craven
ge. With the
tary-manager is
rman C. B. Dean.

By JOHN THOMPSON

YOU have plodded along respectably for years and many people who don't know you very well say you are colourless and worthy and that you excite them less than a glass of water.

When you hardly expect it yourself and no one else does you find success. And with a confirmed belief in your mediocrity many refuse to praise your achievement and promise that it cannot last.

That is how it has been in football with the brave bid for promotion of unfashionable Fulham.

In other sporting centres their success has been admitted grudgingly. I have heard it claimed often that "they're not really a good team—they're in a false position."

Fulham themselves wear the unaccustomed cloak of success as calmly as if they were used to it.

"There's a long way to go yet," says team manager Eddie Perry. "The idea of us playing in the First Division is never discussed at Craven Cottage.

"If we are not promoted we will at least have learnt much which will be helpful to us next season.

DIVISION II

	P	W	D	L	Goals F	Goals A	Pts
South'ton ..	34	21	7	6	66	30	49
Fulham	33	18	7	8	61	32	43
West Brom.	32	18	6	8	52	34	42
Tottenham	34	14	13	7	55	33	41
Cardiff	33	14	10	9	48	41	38
Chesterfield	34	12	13	9	45	40	37

"Our reputation of being in a false position in the League may be because of a spell when we were winning by scraped goals in games which might have gone either way," says Frank Osborne, Fulham's secretary-manager.

"That spasm ended long ago. Since Arthur Rowley came from West Bromwich to lead our attack we have taken twenty points from thirteen games. He has scored eleven goals himself.

"Our system here is never to look at a fixture list. *Each match is judged* separately. That is a lesson from golf. No one can win if he is thinking how difficult the next hole will be. He must concentrate on the hole he is playing."

Trainer Frank Penn has been with Fulham for thirty-two years. For sixteen years he was their outside left. Here he treats an ankle injury received by Jezzard.

Top Wages

Main reason for Fulham's contentment is the feeling of security held by all the players.

More than any club Fulham recruit their staff from their own old footballers. Players know there will be a job for them at Craven Cottage when their days on the field are over. They appreciate that they will not be thrown on the scrap-heap as they would be with clubs which are much wealthier than Fulham.

"They receive top wages and maximum benefits and realise that we are all here to help them," says Osborne. "In return they give us their best. No one needs more."

Osborne is the former Bromley, Tottenham Hotspur and Fulham centre forward.

"Strange how a chance meeting changed my life," he says. Born in South Africa—the son of a British Army *major*—his *playing* career had ended and he was arranging to return to South Africa.

"I happened to meet John Dean, then Fulham chairman, on a Tube station. He asked my plans and suggested I should stay in London and work in his business."

Fifteen years ago Osborne was made a Fulham director. When he became secretary-manager this season he had the advantage of knowing which positions needed strengthening.

He saw his team's first ten games and has watched them only twice since. He contends that his job is finished each Friday after he has discussed plans for the match on the following day.

He knows, too, that he can trust Eddie Perry to advise the team wisely at half-time.

Most of his week-ends this winter Osborne has travelled in search of talent. He has made five trips to Scotland, three to Ireland, and many to the North of England

"It is better to go looking for players when you are doing well rather than leave it until you are failing," he says. "When there is panic in the camp other clubs realise you are *desperate* and *know* you will take chances.

"If you wait to buy until you are in trouble you begin to lose faith in your own judgment."

Few clubs have men on the board who are consciously comedians. Fulham have Tommy Trinder as a director and this is more important than you may think.

Osborne is convinced that the effect of Trinder on the players has helped them win games they would otherwise have lost.

"Apart from believing in him as a mascot they know he is the best possible cure for the common football *affliction of 'butterflies* in the tummy.'" says Osborne

DIRECTOR TRINDER
If it's Promotion you're after
Get Trinder for laughter.

Superstition

"Listening to Tommy on away trips they forget about football completely I sometimes wonder if he doesn't tire the players by making them laugh too much."

The comedian is a superstition with the Fulham team. If he is there they fancy luck will favour them.

Osborne has studied the mental approach to the game more carefully than most managers. He knows it is important.

He has tried to dispel the "bogey team" feeling which haunts all clubs, the feeling that "we always do badly *against so-and-so.*"

"It can only be yourselves which make West Bromwich and Southampton and one or two others Fulham bogey teams," he argues.

"Sometimes," he adds, "they agree with me when *they* go out. Then they hit the cross-bar or have an unlucky goal scored against them and begin to wonder whether there's something in the bogey nonsense after all."

Like most of the happy teams I have met, the Fulham eleven consists mainly of players who cost only their £10 signing-on fee.

Douglas Flack, the goalkeeper, was a boy in the office at sixteen. "All the time his talent was overlooked by us he never *complained,*" *says* Osborne.

"He has followed Fulham since he could walk and I expect *Fulham* will *still* be his club when he is an old man."

Flack's loyalty and enthusiasm are equalled by £10 full backs Harry Freeman and Joe Bacuzzi. Osborne describes Freeman as "one of the hardest kickers of a muddy *ball* I have ever seen."

Freeman came from the Oxfordshire village team of Woodstock. *Once he* was told a First Division manager wanted to buy him. "If I leave Fulham it will be to go back to Woodstock," he said.

In his fifteen years with the club Bacuzzi has known success and failure by the team, and because he has played well through both the crowd have grown to admire him. He is un*questionably their favourite.*

Right half Len Quested is called Tugboat Annie. In the Navy he served in a tugboat at Sydney, Australia. "He never lags," says Osborne. "He has tremendous energy and in his *last few games I am* told his ball-play has improved tremendously."

Jim Taylor, centre half, joined Fulham from a British Legion side as an inside right. "I've not known a better tackler," says Osborne.

He regards left half Pat Beasley as "the cheapest player there has ever been." Huddersfield took *only £750 for him*

Memories

Of Arthur Stevens, outside right, who came from Wimbledon. "He never wastes a ball."

Bob Thomas, £4,000 inside right from Plymouth, is in the Mortensen mould. "His fine bursts of speed with the ball outpace most defenders."

Osborne thinks Bedford Jezzard—named after an uncle's public house—"a really promising player."

Fulham's only big-money star is outside left John McDonald, for whom £12,000 was paid to Bournemouth. He is often dangerous, a potential match-winner on his own.

There you have some of the players who have *brought a fame supporters* never expected to see at their little riverside club.

Nearly all these young men have happy memories *of Jack Peart, the manager* who looked after them until last autumn.

Carried On

In the little parish pump world of Soccer there is sometimes malice and occasionally double-dealing but in the years I knew him I never heard an unkind word said about Peart nor did I hear him say one.

Frank Osborne was recalling yesterday how, through the weeks when he was in hospital dying, Peart would worry about his team and share fully in their happiness when *they won.*

"Only a day or two before he died there was a little note from him reminding us that he had promised trials *to some local boys and ask*ing us to make sure that they were well looked after."

I believe Jack Peart would be proud of the way they *have carried on his work at* Craven Cottage

nearest rival, Dixie Dean, who "only" managed 379. The shame was that he only played one further season for Fulham.

Rowley's goals, combined with excellent play from the likes of Joe Bacuzzi, Thomas, Stevens, Len Quested and Jim Taylor saw Fulham home. The team won six of their last seven games to take the title, using third-choice keeper Larry Gage for the last three.

Some of the men who are trying to take Fulham into the First Division. Players from left to right are Thomas, S., Quested, Stevens, Wallbanks, Bewley, Taylor, Thomas, B., Bacuzzi, Beasley, Freeman, Flack and Eddie Perry (team-manager).

Division One 1949–50

In the end, Fulham's first season in the First Division could be considered a success. On 18th February all was well. Fulham were 13th in the league and Len Quested had received an England 'B' call-up. They beat a depleted Blackpool side (missing Matthews, Mortensen, and four other regulars) 1-0 at the Cottage thanks to a goal from Bob Thomas, drew their next three games, then went on an extraordinarily bad run, losing eight of their last 10 and missing relegation by only five points.

Fulham forward Jack McDonald plants a penalty kick past Charlton goalkeeper Sam Bartram at the Valley on New Year's Eve 1949. Fulham lost 2-1.

Bedford Jezzard's header goes over the bar.

Fulham goalkeeper Hugh Kelly claims the ball.

Hugh Kelly pounces to thwart a Manchester United chance, accompanied by Joe Bacuzzi, Jim Taylor and Pat Beasley. Fulham won 1-0, the team's big scalp in the First Division that year. Bedford Jezzard got the winner, 35,362 watched. Fulham's Arthur Rowley played against his brother, United's Jack, for the first time in a league match.

Jim Taylor joined Fulham from a British Legion side in 1938. At that point he played inside-right, but was converted to a centre-half. Taylor was an influential player in Fulham's 1948–49 Second Division Championship season, and played 261 times for Fulham between 1946 and 1953.

Frank Osborne enthused that "I've not known a better tackler." Bill Dodgin went further: "He's a shrewd student of soccer and an example to the rest of the players both on and off the field. And I still believe he's the best centre-half in England."

Captain Jim Taylor, New Year's Day 1950.

1950–51 *Attempting to Consolidate in Division One*

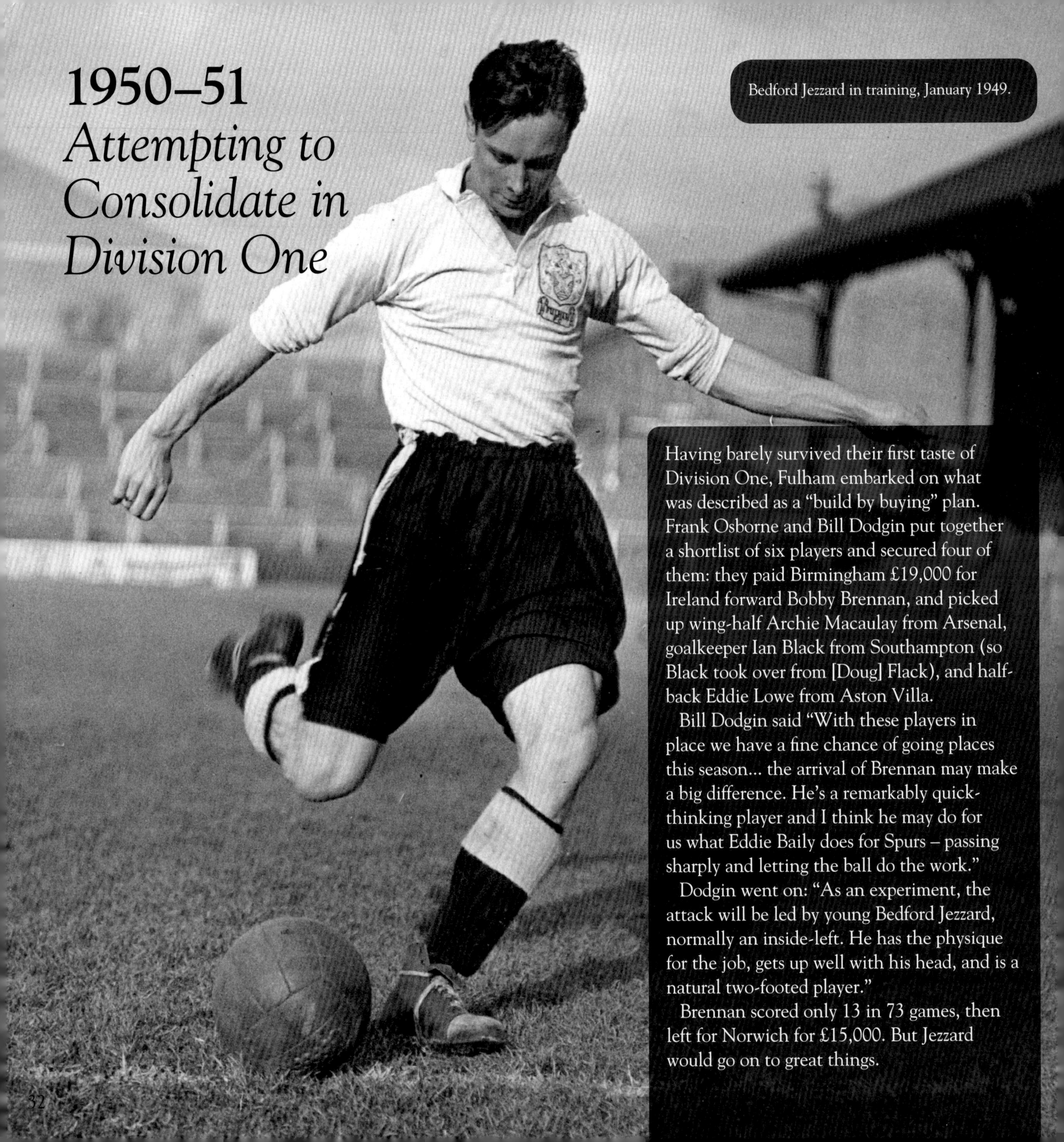

Bedford Jezzard in training, January 1949.

Having barely survived their first taste of Division One, Fulham embarked on what was described as a "build by buying" plan. Frank Osborne and Bill Dodgin put together a shortlist of six players and secured four of them: they paid Birmingham £19,000 for Ireland forward Bobby Brennan, and picked up wing-half Archie Macaulay from Arsenal, goalkeeper Ian Black from Southampton (so Black took over from [Doug] Flack), and half-back Eddie Lowe from Aston Villa.

Bill Dodgin said "With these players in place we have a fine chance of going places this season... the arrival of Brennan may make a big difference. He's a remarkably quick-thinking player and I think he may do for us what Eddie Baily does for Spurs – passing sharply and letting the ball do the work."

Dodgin went on: "As an experiment, the attack will be led by young Bedford Jezzard, normally an inside-left. He has the physique for the job, gets up well with his head, and is a natural two-footed player."

Brennan scored only 13 in 73 games, then left for Norwich for £15,000. But Jezzard would go on to great things.

–LEGENDS–

Bedford Jezzard

Bedford Jezzard came to Fulham from Watford in 1948, and stayed for 16 years. He was a successful centre-forward, particularly in the Second Division, where he scored 124 in four seasons after the team was relegated in 1952. His playing career ended in 1956, but after spending time as Fulham's youth team manager, Jezzard found himself in charge of the first team. Fulham won promotion in his first season in charge, and stayed up for five seasons after that. He walked out on Fulham and football after behind-the-scenes issues became too much to put up with.

Jezzard in training, 1955.

BELOW: The Thatched House pub, Dalling Road, Hammersmith. Jezzard ran the pub after he left football.

B. JEZZARD. LICENSED TO SELL WINES, SPIRITS, BEERS, AND TOBACCO ON AND OFF PREMISES.

FOOTBALL –STATS–

Bedford Jezzard

Name: Bedford Jezzard

Born: London 1927

Died: London 2005

Position: Centre-forward

Fulham playing career: 1948–1956

Fulham manager: 1958–1964

Club appearances: 306

Goals: 155

England appearances: 2

Goals: 0

Fulham's expensive new signings took some time to get going, relying on a few rare spurts of form throughout the season to earn the points needed to stay up.

Before the Arsenal away game in late November, manager Bill Dodgin approached Archie Macaulay, who had signed from Arsenal. "This week's pre-match team talk is all yours," he said. "You know more about Arsenal than any of us so tell us what you think and we'll exchange ideas."

Macaulay seems to have taken his task seriously. First he placed a strip of canvas on the dressing room floor. He marked out a football field on the canvas and onto this laid 22 pieces of wood, hewn from a broom handle, representing the teams' 22 players. Then he explained how Arsenal could be beaten, moving the wooden pieces around as he talked. His team-mates listened intently.

Then Arsenal won 5-1, with Doug Lishman (one of the game's forgotten stars) scoring three goals.

A 1-1 draw at the Cottage with Newcastle, March 1951.

This season also saw the beginnings of something special. Bobby Robson made his debut away at Sheffield Wednesday (by his own admission he had a terrible game, and wasn't picked again until midway through the following season), and Fulham signed a promising schoolboy from Edmonton, North London: Johnny Haynes.

These lads find the Cottage makes the happiest of homes

By WILLIE EVANS

EDDIE PERRY, who is in charge of juniors at Craven Cottage, accomplished a personal triumph when he persuaded fifteen-year-old Johnny Haynes to join Fulham. Haynes, who comes from Edmonton, jumped to prominence following a brilliant display at inside forward for England Schoolboys who trounced Scotland at Wembley earlier this year.

One of the factors which influenced young Johnny's decision to join Fulham was a chat he had with two boys already enrolled there—L. Caretta, of Islington, and T. Chamberlain, another schoolboy international who was Haynes's team-mate.

Other famous clubs wanted Johnny. Arsenal have had a report on Haynes in their files for the past two seasons. Spurs, Portsmouth and Wolves were also anxious to get him.

But there is something about Fulham which attracts the lads. Maybe it is the atmosphere or the friendly relationship which exists between the staff, the recognised star players, and the boys who have still to make their way.

Almost a hundred ungsters have written asking for trials. They will get a chance to show their ability in games arranged for August 14 and 15.

I believe that a few seasons from now Fulham will have groomed a bunch of boys smart enough to take their place in top-class Soccer. And I think also, that Craven Cottage lads will come to know their ground as "Happy Cottage."

THEY WILL BE TOGETHER AGAIN

Goalkeeper Roy Milton, 47, who played in Torquay United's Southern League side last season, has signed amateur forms for Bury. He rejoins Mr. John McNeill, manager of Bury, and formerly in charge at Torquay who discovered Milton

A young Johnny Haynes in training, August 1954.

1951–52 *Bottom of the Table: Relegated*

The 1951–52 season was a disaster. Fulham lost their first four games and another six straight in October (the City game pictured was the fifth of these defeats).

That run ended in November with a 2-2 draw against Aston Villa. The side was 2-0 down when Bill Dodgin left his seat to make a change. The crowd "gave him the bird, loud, long and clear. It was malicious." The players, incensed by the incident, fought back to draw the game.

Frank Firth, one of the fans who booed Dodgin, felt so bad about the incident that he called the manager and was invited over for a chat. The two men talked for three hours. Dodgin noted that "as a good supporter of the club, Frank had a right to have his questions answered. Within the limits of club security, I tried to answer all of them." Firth felt better, too: "I am not ashamed of booing Mr Dodgin. I think that is the only way a club supporter can voice his displeasure. Now that I know Fulham's problems I am sorry to have had any part of it [the booing]. I now have a very great regard for the manager."

This was no turning point though, and while form improved slightly, Fulham finished bottom and were relegated to Division Two.

November 1951: Bert Trautmann in the City goal punches clear as Geoff Taylor challenges. Fulham lost 2-1.

City's Don Revie clears the danger.

–LEGENDS–

Charlie Mitten

PAGE 16 DAILY MIRROR Monday December 5, 1955

Mirror SPORT 4 PAGES

THIS IS HOW TO DO IT, CHARLIE

My run up is letting me down, says Mitten after third penalty miss

★ PERSONALITY PAGE —conducted by FRANK McGHEE

CHARLIE MITTEN, Fulham left winger, is the spot-kick sure-shot who missed only ONE penalty in FIFTEEN years with Manchester United.

Charlie is the footballer who once said, "A penalty should ALWAYS mean a goal."

Yet the last-minute penalty he hit against a post in the 2—1 defeat by Sheffield Wednesday was the THIRD he has missed in succession.

Mitten is his own sternest critic. He says: "I still maintain a professional should always score from the spot, and I admit I should have done.

"But I think I know what is wrong. I have been veering too much to one side in my run-up."

Will he take any more penalties? "If they are vital ones, Yes. It would be unfair to place the burden on someone new if the match depends on it."

Look at that picture on the right, Charlie . . . that's the way it's done by Everton centre half Tommy Jones, beating Chelsea's Bill Robertson.

One bright spot in the season was the arrival of the legendary Charlie Mitten. Mitten had been a Manchester United player under Sir Matt Busby, scoring 61 goals in 161 appearances from outside-left. But on a tour of the USA Mitten had received an offer he couldn't refuse: Bogotá Santa Fé of Colombia were prepared to offer him £5,000 to sign, then £5,000 a year to play. He was on around £10 a week in England, so the decision, in some respects, was not difficult.

Mitten was a great success in Colombia, but soon had another offer: Spain's Real Madrid wanted him. Alfredo Di Stéfano and Héctor Rial (both playing in the Colombian league at the time) were also courted. The latter two did make the move, but Mitten and his wife decided to return to England. Had he gone to Madrid he'd have been part of that side's amazing European Cup success; as it was he was disciplined by the English FA and Manchester United, banned for six months and put on the transfer list (United still held his registration). Two teams came in for him: Huddersfield Town and Fulham.

When Mitten joined in January, Fulham had won only one of their preceding 15 games.

Mitten's first match was a 2-1 defeat at Chelsea, but two weeks later they thrashed Middlesbrough 6-0. A week after that they beat West Bromwich, but the resurgence ended as suddenly as it had begun, and Fulham sank without a trace. Mitten managed six goals in 16 games that season, and went on to score 33 in 160 in his Fulham career.

Mitten was a fabulous player and Fulham were lucky that circumstances made him available to them. But arguably, the team didn't make the most of his presence. While Mitten enjoyed his time at Fulham, he was frustrated, too. He rightly enthused about the talent the team was able to put on the field. With Johnny Haynes, Bedford Jezzard, Bobby Robson and Arthur Stevens working up front with him, the side was not short of attacking flair. But all this attack put a lot of pressure on the defence, and the team was never quite balanced enough to fulfil its potential. Mitten also felt that the Bill Dodgin and Frank Osborne management combination didn't always work out, with Dodgin nominally in charge of the team but frequently (Mitten thought) undermined.

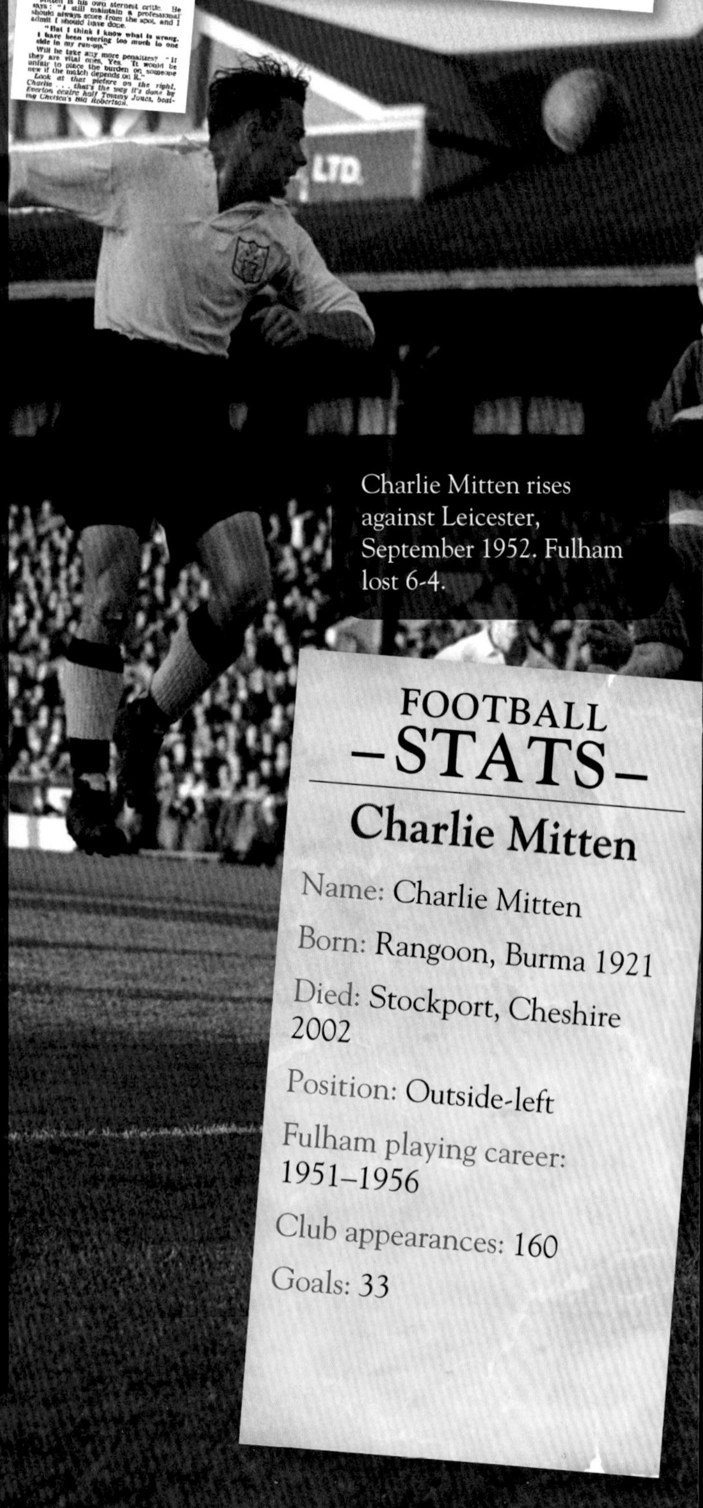

Charlie Mitten rises against Leicester, September 1952. Fulham lost 6-4.

FOOTBALL –STATS–

Charlie Mitten

Name: Charlie Mitten

Born: Rangoon, Burma 1921

Died: Stockport, Cheshire 2002

Position: Outside-left

Fulham playing career: 1951–1956

Club appearances: 160

Goals: 33

–LEGENDS–

Johnny Haynes

If 1951–52 was disappointing, 1952–53 saw the debut of Johnny Haynes.

Haynes, who lived near the Spurs ground, had shown great promise while playing for England schoolboys, and Arsenal, Spurs, Portsmouth and Wolves (then a fine side) were all interested in him. But Haynes chose Fulham. He went on to play 658 times for the club, scoring 158 goals.

There is no doubt that Haynes is Fulham's greatest ever player, and probably always will be. These days a talent like his would probably leave for one of the game's giants, where he might challenge for the serious trophies and where he would receive a salary beyond Fulham's means.

Things were different then, though, and besides, Haynes was far from underpaid. On the contrary: when the maximum wage was lifted Tommy Trinder, with typical ostentatiousness, made Haynes the highest paid footballer in the country. He deserved it.

Bobby Robson, on Haynes' death, said "he was a wonderful passer of the ball, one of the best I've seen and I've been in football 50 years". Sven Goran Eriksson compared him to Roberto Mancini (curiously, Mancini scored 156 goals in 545 games, a ratio not dissimilar to Haynes' record). Bobby Charlton was a huge admirer, and as a youngster had been told to model his game on Haynes. Johnny Giles went to see Haynes in 1960 and said: "the sheer intelligence of his football glowed through the night and on the bus home I replayed his every move... today we talk about power and speed and we ask if the great players of yesterday could operate in these conditions. Well, let me tell you something; if Haynes stepped into a game today he would be seen as someone from another planet. He would be a man from Mars. Nutrition, training practices, physical development, all these things change. But some things don't, and they include speed of thought and technique. That so often today is the missing element, technique – sheer technique. Haynes had so much of it, allied with intelligence and vision, it was ridiculous."

Haynes played for England 56 times and scored 18 goals, captaining the side in between the Billy Wright and Bobby Moore eras. Fulham's Stevenage Road Stand has been renamed in his memory, and a fine statue of him stands outside the stadium's gates.

FOOTBALL –STATS–

Johnny Haynes

Name: Johnny Haynes

Born: Edmonton, Middlesex 1934

Died: Edinburgh 2005

Position: Inside-forward

Fulham playing career: 1952–1970

Club appearances: 658

Goals: 158

England appearances: 56

Goals: 18

ABOVE: Johnny Haynes warms up before the October 1955 game against Doncaster. Fulham lost 4-2, Haynes and Robson scored.

Haynes and his pet budgie, Bimbo.

Haynes signs autographs in October 1955.

Haynes captains England against Scotland, April 1961. Here he talks to HRH the Duke of Edinburgh. England won 9-3; Haynes scored two goals.

Haynes leads out his team.

1952–58

From 1952–53 to 1957–58 Fulham consolidated, finishing halfway up Division Two more often than not. But the next great Fulham team was growing: Bobby Robson and Jimmy Hill made their debuts in 1951, Charlie Mitten and Johnny Haynes made theirs in 1952, Trevor Chamberlain in 1954, Roy Bentley in 1956, and 1957 brought Jimmy Langley, George Cohen and Tony Macedo. Graham Leggat arrived in 1958, Alan Mullery in 1959.

LEFT: Fulham, September 1956.

Jimmy Hill challenges against Liverpool, October 1956. Fulham lost 4-3.

-LEGENDS-

Roy Bentley

Awkward this as Bentley is a legitimate Chelsea legend, having captained that side to their first ever league title in 1954–55. However, his impact at Fulham was significant, too.

George Cohen was full of praise for Bentley's influence: "He had dropped into the Second Division with Fulham and moved back to right-half – just in front of me. He was a marvellous guide, taking me through the thickets of professional football."

Alan Mullery, talking about his debut, noted that while the rest of the team were busy with their routines, Bentley came over to reassure him, promising to talk him through the game. "When the game started, Roy Bentley kept his promise and talked to me non-stop. 'Pick him up, Alan… don't let him go… push him wide… stay with him. Outside left… he's free… hit him with the ball… good pass, son!'"

If Bentley was a father figure for young players, he was a force of nature for opponents, capable of dominating games from midfield.

His Fulham career took a while to get going, first because Chelsea wouldn't sell him at a price Fulham could pay. Bristol City made an offer, but the player refused as his heart was set on Fulham. This left Bentley in limbo for a time, before Chelsea eventually let him go.

Despite scoring on his debut (September 1956), his early games at Fulham weren't as successful as had been hoped, something manager Dugald Livingstone put down to his "trying too hard. He's so eager to justify himself after sticking his neck out for Fulham when on the Chelsea transfer list that his confidence is being affected." Bentley stayed in a forward role until November 1957, then spent the rest of his career either at right-half or centre-half, filling in at centre-forward on occasion.

FOOTBALL
-STATS-

Roy Bentley

Name: Roy Bentley

Born: Bristol 1924

Position: Various

Fulham playing career: 1956–1961

Club appearances: 158

Goals: 25

England appearances: 12

Goals: 9

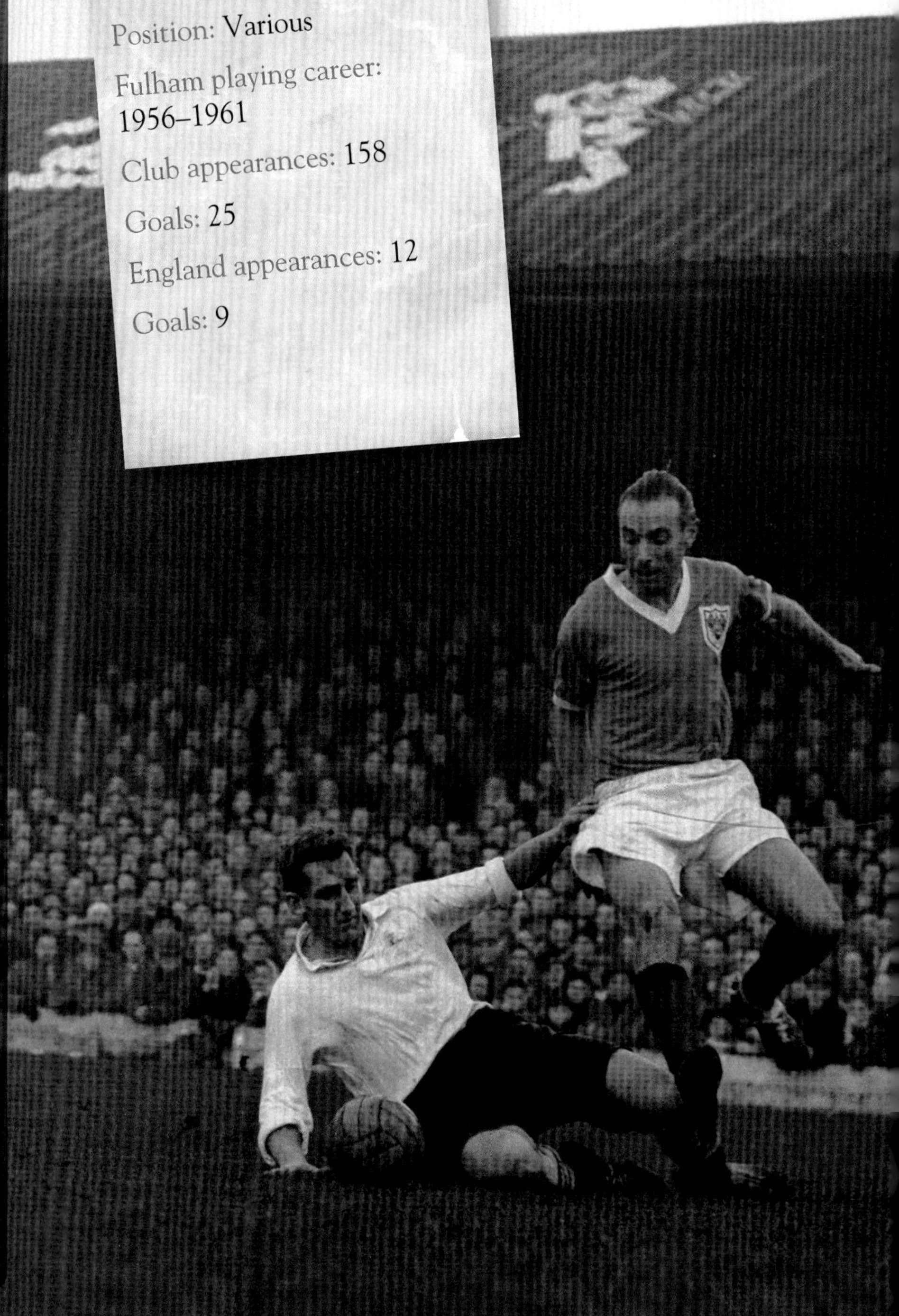

Roy Bentley tackles Stanley Matthews, January 1957. Fulham lost 6-2.

February 1958: Johnny Haynes goes for goal in a 2-2 draw with West Ham, as Jimmy Hill looks on. Maurice Cook started up front, having signed from Watford for £15,000 the day before.

FULHAM FOOTBALL & ATHLETIC CO. LTD
CRAVEN COTTAGE

Wembley: So Near, So Far

The 1957–58 season was dominated by Fulham's run to the FA Cup semi-final.

Having beaten Yeovil Town in the Third Round, Fulham were drawn against Charlton Athletic, then going well in Division Two, in the Fourth.

Charlton had the better of the game but Tony Macedo was playing a blinder in the Fulham goal. Jimmy Hill put Fulham ahead in the 66th minute, a lead held until the last kick of the game. Macedo took a goal-kick short to Roy Bentley, whose pass to Arthur Stevens was intercepted, Charlton broke at speed and John Ryan hammered home an equalizer.

Bentley more than made up for it in the replay, putting in a performance that was "the inspiration behind Fulham's Cup replay win". Bentley dominated the match, making the penalty area his "almost exclusive property – headed and kicked away, tackled and shouted advice like a man inspired". Further to this, he scored one and made another as Fulham won 2-0.

Fulham fans queue for FA Cup Fourth Round tickets outside Craven Cottage.

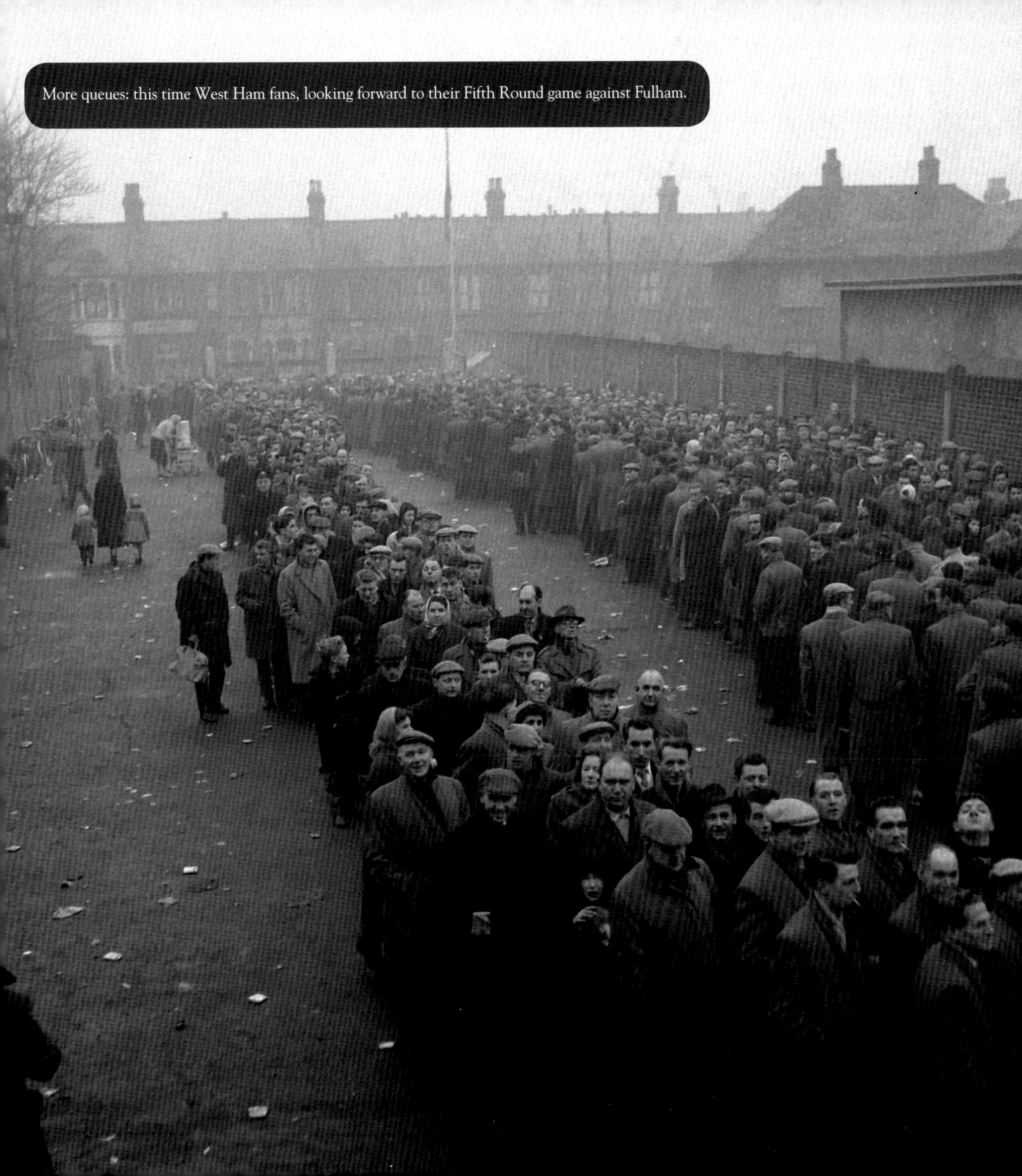

More queues: this time West Ham fans, looking forward to their Fifth Round game against Fulham.

Tony Macedo saves acrobatically.

Fulham drew West Ham in the Fifth Round, and won an entertaining game 3-2. Roy Dwight made it 1-0 to Fulham with a neat lob, but West Ham equalized through Mike Grice, then went ahead with a John Bond penalty after a spectacular foul in the area.

Jimmy Hill pulled it back to 2-2, arriving late at the far post, then Haynes won the match with a terrific opportunist finish, chasing Chamberlain's pass then sliding to divert the ball across the goalkeeper. It trickled slowly across the Upton Park mud into the bottom corner, a dramatic winner.

ABOVE: A young Fulham fan with a quarter-final ticket.

The Sixth Round draw gave Fulham a home tie against Bristol Rovers. "We are all absolutely delighted," said manager Livingstone.

Fulham won 3-1, Haynes setting up Hill for the first with an inch-perfect pass. Arthur Stevens made it two following a seven-man passing move, and added another before half-time. Rovers came back strongly in the second half, scored one and then hit the bar, but Macedo was again in form and Fulham were through. After the game Johnny Haynes' mother revealed that her son had worn the same lucky suit on every Cup day that season.

Tosh Chamberlain goes for goal against Bristol Rovers.

FOOTBALL
-STATS-

Arthur Stevens

Name: Arthur Stevens

Born: London 1921

Died: Epsom, Surrey 2007

Position: Outside-right

Fulham playing career: 1946–1959

Club appearances: 413

Goals: 124

-LEGENDS-

Arthur Stevens

Arthur Stevens – nicknamed Pablo because of his dark complexion – was a one-club man. George Cohen says that Stevens was one of the most skilful players he ever saw, as good as Stanley Matthews. Stevens was strong in the air, had two good feet, and was lightning quick over 15 yards. He played 413 games for Fulham and scored 124 goals.

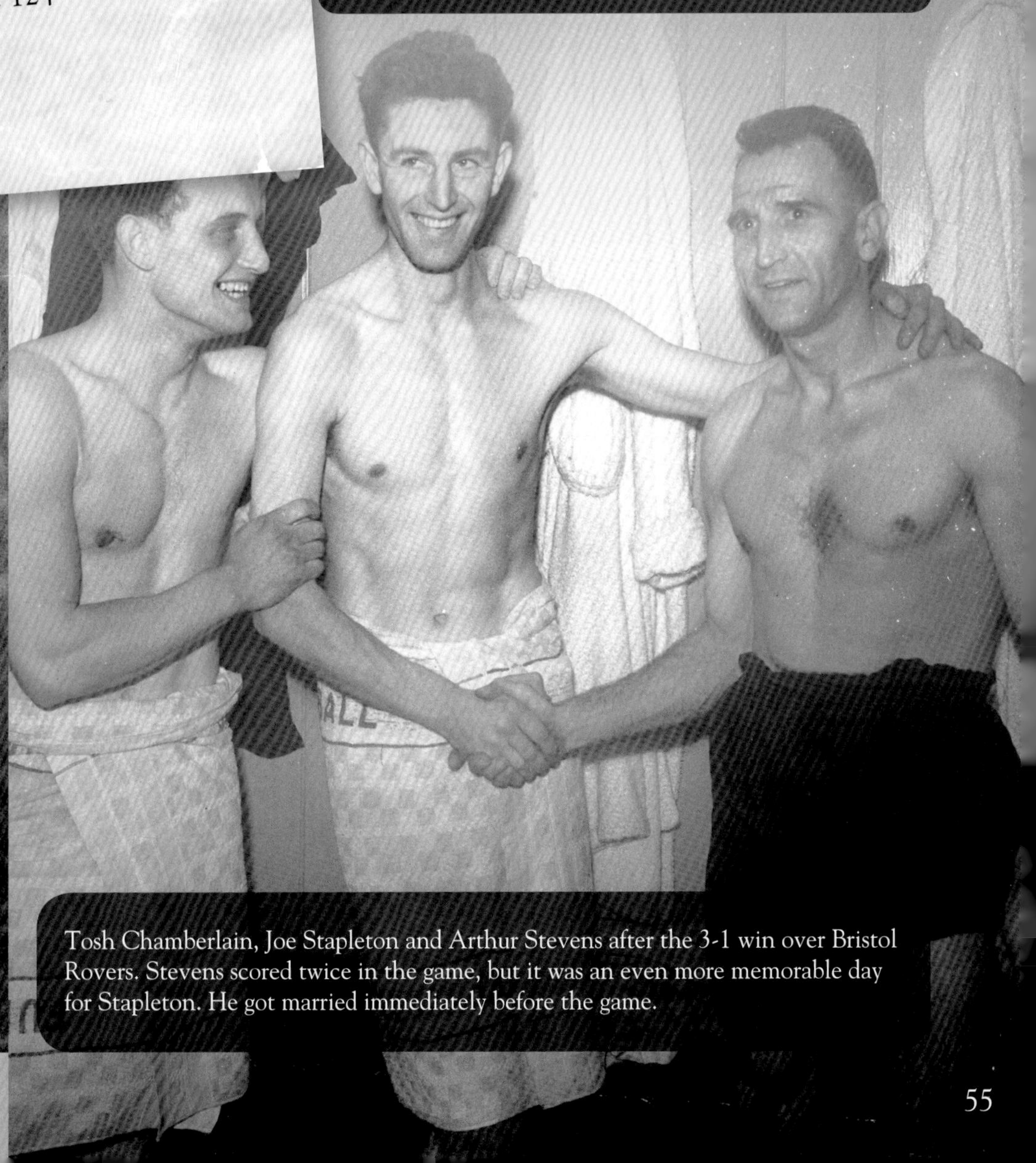

Tosh Chamberlain, Joe Stapleton and Arthur Stevens after the 3-1 win over Bristol Rovers. Stevens scored twice in the game, but it was an even more memorable day for Stapleton. He got married immediately before the game.

RIGHT: March 1958: the midnight queue for FA Cup semi-final tickets outside Craven Cottage.

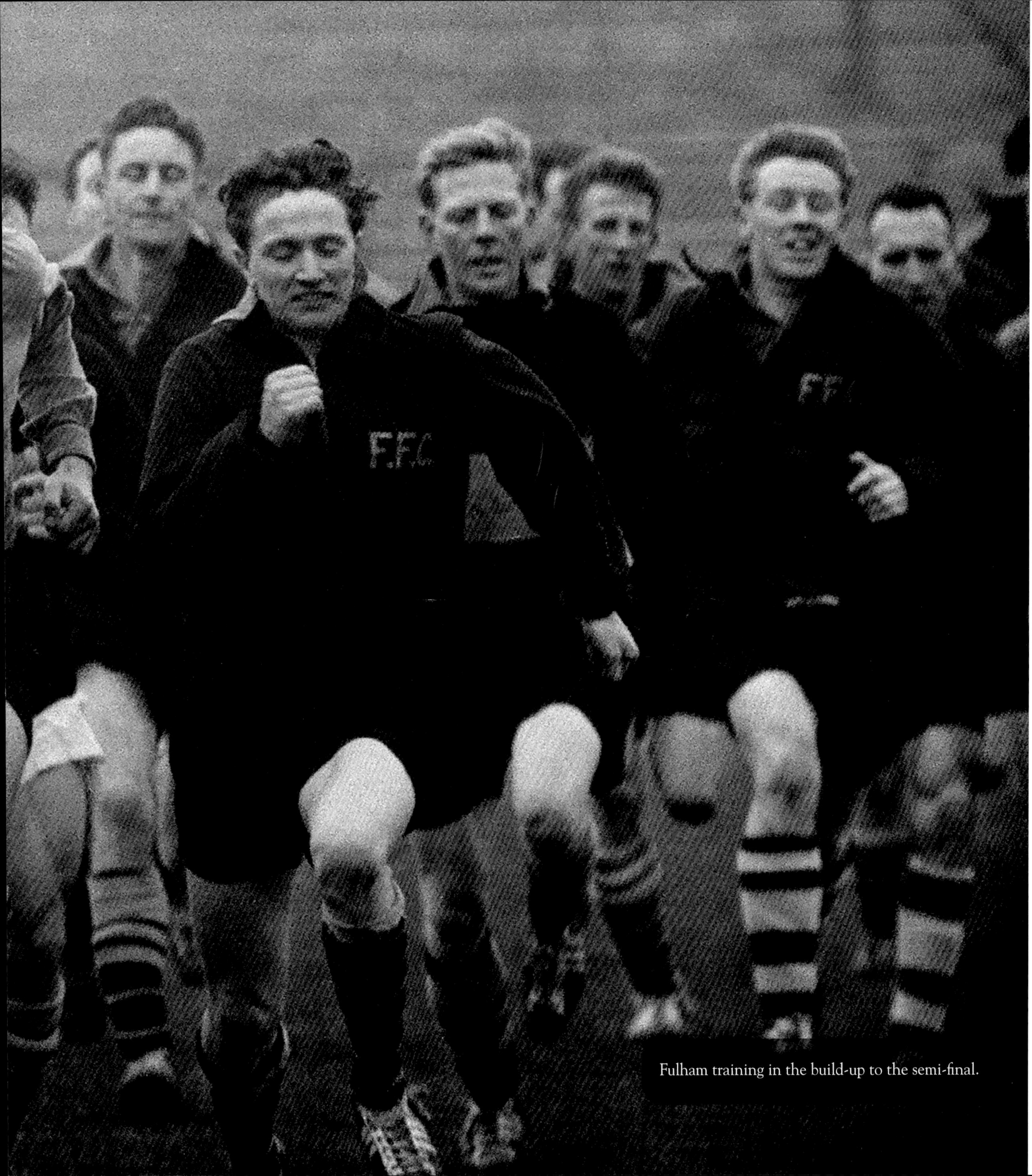

Fulham training in the build-up to the semi-final.

The semi-final brought the mighty Manchester United into Fulham's path. George Cohen noted that this was something more than an important football match, Fulham cast as "the other team" against a United side so crushed in Munich only weeks earlier.

In the event Tony Macedo performed miracles and Johnny Haynes played "probably the greatest game of his life", and the Whites managed a 2-2 draw, all the more creditable because Jimmy Langley seriously injured himself in the first half (these were the days before substitutes). Bobby Charlton scored first, Arthur Stevens levelled, Jimmy Hill put Fulham ahead, then Charlton scored again on the brink of half-time. The second half had just as much action but no goals, the two goalkeepers saving everything that came their way.

Macedo had been magnificent, but football can be a cruel game, and he had a disaster in the replay.

United score in the semi-final.

United scored first when Macedo was drawn out of position, allowing Colin Webster to find Alex Dawson for a diving header. Stevens equalized following a sweet pass from Haynes, but then Macedo's jitters struck again: Dawson struck a shot from the edge of the area, Macedo got both hands to it, but the ball slipped through him and into the net. Chamberlain made it 2-2, but Macedo wasn't finished, taking his eye off a clearance and so presenting Shay Brennan with an open goal. 3-2.

Dawson completed his hat-trick following some Charlton wizardry, but back came Fulham, and Roy Dwight made it 4-3. Haynes had a fourth disallowed for hand-ball, then Charlton wrapped it up with a screaming fifth.

Action from the replay.

United and Fulham players leave the field together at the end of the semi-final.

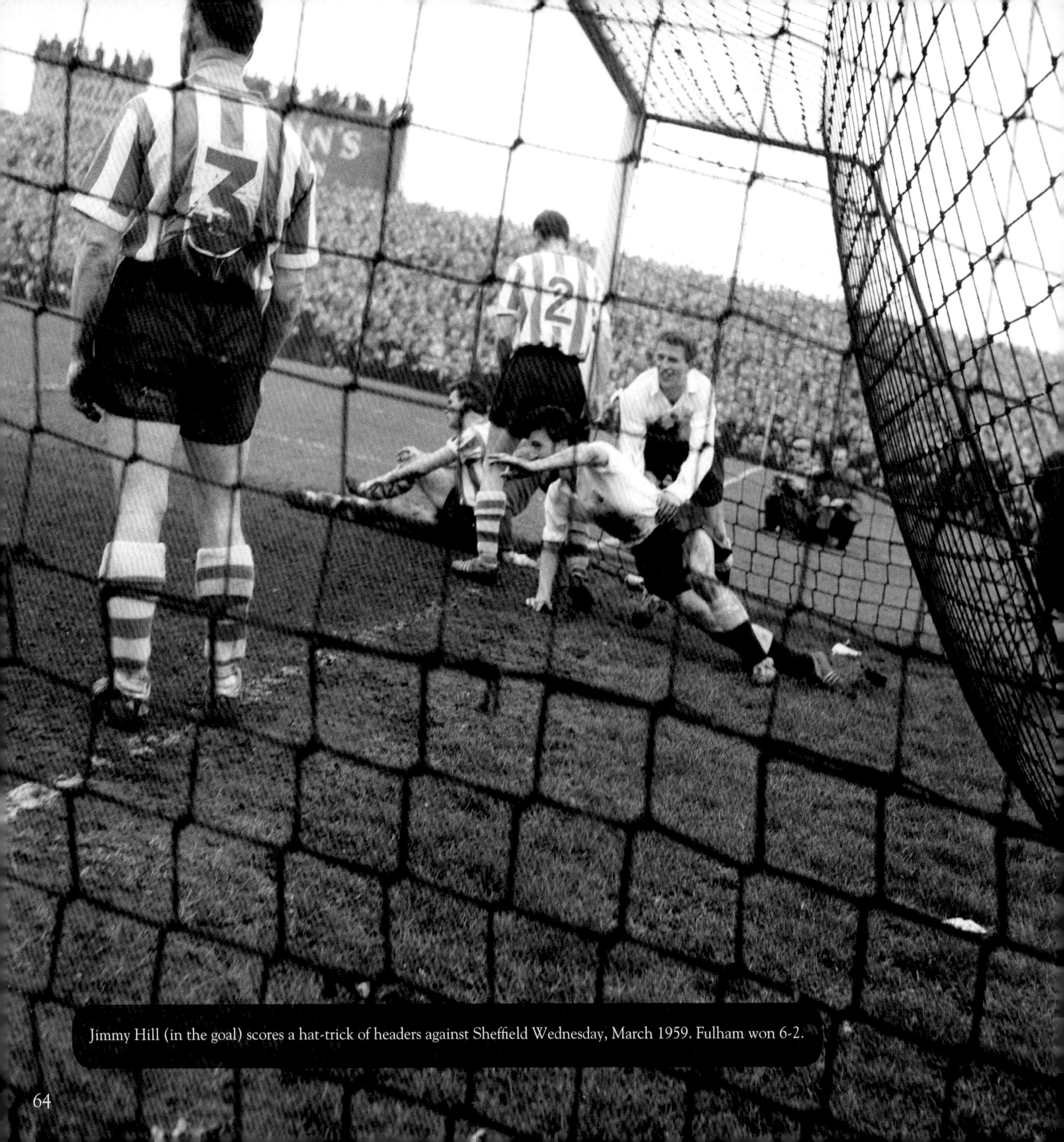

Jimmy Hill (in the goal) scores a hat-trick of headers against Sheffield Wednesday, March 1959. Fulham won 6-2.

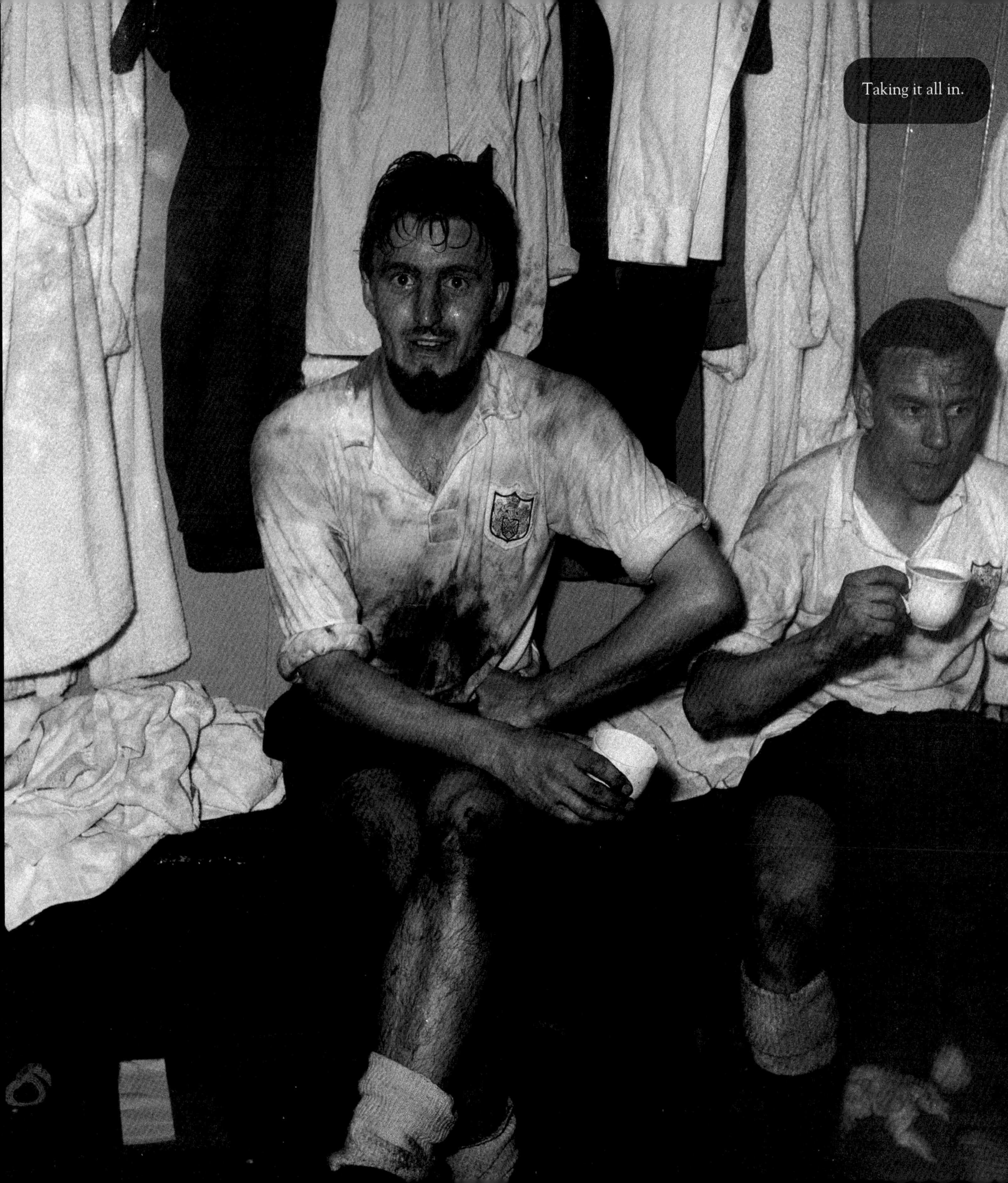

Taking it all in.

1958–59 *The Start of Something Good: Promotion*

Fulham's Cup form from the previous season spilled over into the next league campaign. They topped the table as late as mid-April, only for Sheffield Wednesday to pip them to the post. No matter: promotion was secure. Fulham were back.

FOOTBALL –STATS–

Graham Leggat

Name: Graham Leggat

Born: Aberdeen 1934

Position: Right-wing/striker

Fulham playing career: 1958–1967

Club appearances: 280

Goals: 134

Scotland appearances: 18

Goals: 8

–LEGENDS–

Graham Leggat

Graham Leggat's Fulham career started with a bang. The club won the first six games of the 1958–59 season, scoring 23 goals in the process. Leggat scored in every match, and went on to notch 21 in 36 appearances that season. In total he scored 134 goals in 277 Fulham games, especially impressive given that most of these were scored in Division One.

In this sense he is one of the club's most important players: Fulham were promoted in his first season, stayed up one way or another for the remainder of his Fulham career, then went down the season after he was sold. Leggat had been similarly influential at Aberdeen at the beginning of his career, helping them to the 1954–55 Scottish League title. All considered, he was one of football's unheralded stars.

Leggat also scored on his Scotland debut, a big dipping volley from 20 yards that put Scotland ahead against a strongly favoured England. Johnny Haynes equalized in the last minute. Leggat went on to score eight goals in 18 caps.

Leggat leaves the field after a 1-0 Cup win over Port Vale, February 1962.

1959–60 *Back in the First Division*

Fulham were back in the top division with a skilful, young team. They were belted 4-0 by Blackburn in the season's first game (Roy Bentley played with a broken nose), but rebounded well with wins over Manchester City and Blackpool. Then came the season's real surprise: mighty Wolves, defending Champions and unbeaten in 18 games running back to the previous February, were beaten 3-1. John Doherty scored through a crowded area, Maurice Cook made it two from 30 yards, and Alf Stokes made it 3-0 in the second half. Wolves pulled one back, but Fulham held on for a fabulous win. There was to be a twist in the tail, though: when the teams played again a week later Wolves won 9-0.

Undeterred, the Whites went unbeaten in October, including a 4-2 win over Birmingham in which Johnny Haynes played a starring role. "The easy accuracy with which Haynes placed pin-point passes to the toes of his team-mates drew murmurs of awe and then roars of applause from the crowd," said the *Daily Mirror*. Bedford Jezzard added: "It's beyond understanding that England can overlook him. He just doesn't have an equal."

Johnny Haynes carries Alf Stokes in pre-season training as the team builds up for its return to Division One.

Chamberlain airborne in pre-season training.

BELOW: Back in the big time: away to Manchester United in November 1959. Fulham got a 3-3 draw thanks to a Leggat hat-trick. Chamberlain and Leggat watch United's Bill Foulkes.

LEFT: A dog runs onto the pitch.

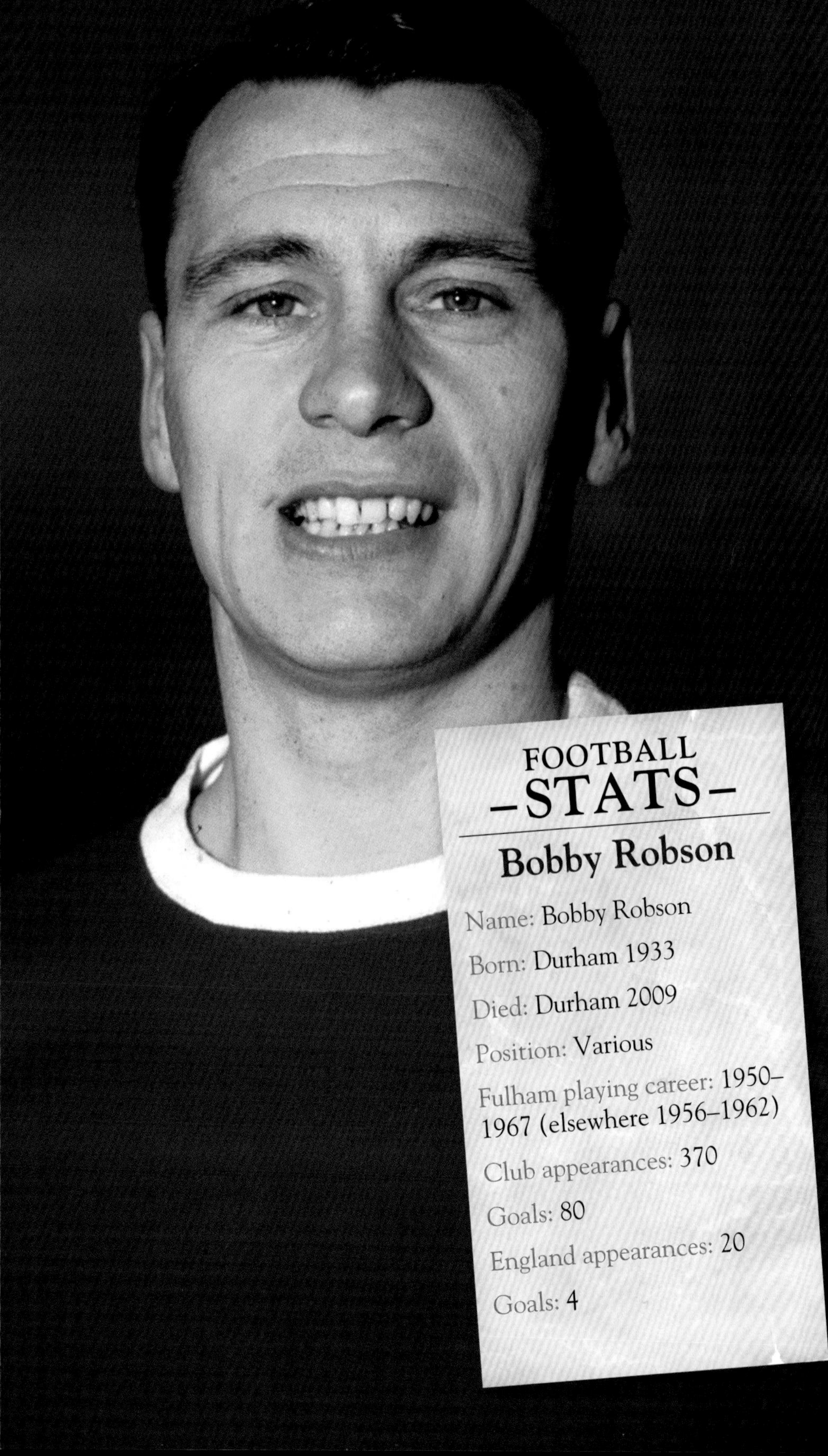

–LEGENDS–

Bobby Robson

Bobby Robson was on Middlesbrough's books as a schoolboy, supported Newcastle, but chose to sign his first professional contract with faraway Fulham. Bill Dodgin Snr offered good money and promised greater opportunities, and Fulham's reputation for giving youth a chance won out. Sure enough, before his 18th birthday Robson made his debut in a 2-2 draw at Sheffield Wednesday.

Robson was a wing-half, and liked to ghost into the area to get on the end of Fulham's attacking moves. As a younger player his eye for goal was impressive, scoring 69 times in 157 games in his first stint at the club.

In 1956 he left Fulham, signing for West Bromwich Albion, then a fine side. He did well there, but didn't win anything, to his lasting regret. Robson returned to Fulham in 1962 and played an important role in keeping Fulham in the First Division for so long. He retired in 1967 to begin a fine coaching career (including a brief, difficult stint at Fulham).

FOOTBALL –STATS–

Bobby Robson

Name: Bobby Robson

Born: Durham 1933

Died: Durham 2009

Position: Various

Fulham playing career: 1950–1967 (elsewhere 1956–1962)

Club appearances: 370

Goals: 80

England appearances: 20

Goals: 4

Bobby Robson, New Year's Day 1960.

ABOVE: Spurs on the attack.

RIGHT: Jimmy Hill celebrates Fulham's goal in a 5-1 defeat at White Hart Lane.

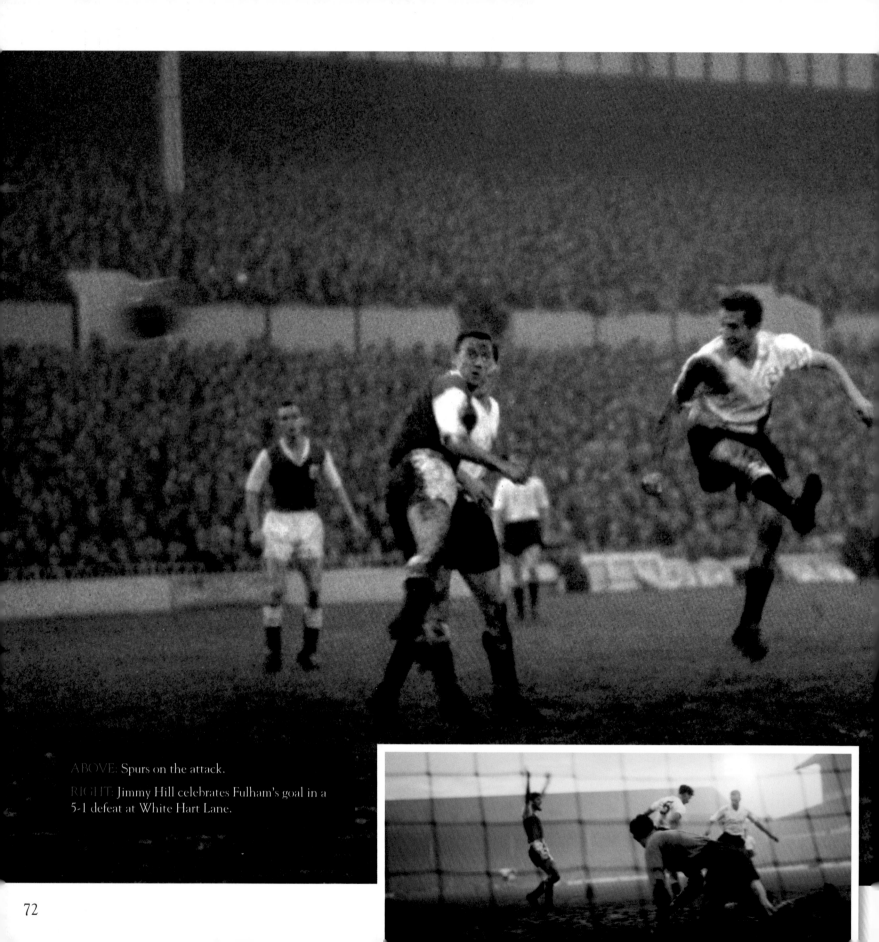

ABOVE: Haynes in unfamiliar blue.

1960–61 *Finding Their Feet*

While prone to the odd thrashing (losing 7-2 to Newcastle, 5-1 to Spurs and Blackburn, 6-1 to Sheffield Wednesday), Fulham had another solid season, getting a number of good wins on the board early on. Graham Leggat was in tremendous form again, scoring 23 in 36 games, including nine in a five-game stretch in October/November.

Johnny Haynes crashed his car in January 1961, breaking a bone in his right hand and receiving stitches for a head wound. Tosh Chamberlain and Roy Bentley were also in the car, Bentley suffering concussion. Haynes missed the club's next game, which was the 6-1 Sheffield Wednesday defeat. In his place was 18-year-old Stan Brown, who made his debut. The *Daily Mirror* felt sorry for him: "Stanley didn't disgrace himself. But it is a mistake to thrust youngsters into a struggling side" (this was one of six consecutive defeats). But Brown went on to have a long and successful career with Fulham.

Meanwhile, there were rumblings behind the scenes about Haynes' occasionally severe captaincy. "If they want a captain who will say nothing on the field they can start right now looking for someone else. That's just not my way." Asked if he had asked for a transfer, Haynes answered "No comment."

March 1961, a 0-0 draw with Spurs.

Jimmy Hill and the End of the Maximum Wage

Jimmy Hill was a better player than he was given credit for, scoring 52 goals in 297 Fulham appearances, but it was off the field that he made his greatest impact on the game. As Chairman of the Professional Footballers Association (PFA), he fought for the abolition of the maximum wage (then £20 a week) and for players' freedom to negotiate new contracts (at the time, contracts were renewed season by season at clubs' discretion).

A post-war boom in football attendance had made a significant amount of money for the clubs' owners, but that had not filtered down to the players. Hill took the players to the brink of a strike to change this, eventually getting his way. One of the first beneficiaries of this was Johnny Haynes. AC Milan had bid £100,000 for Haynes, and Chairman Tommy Trinder had rejected that offer, adding that if the club had the power, they would pay him £100 a week. Trinder probably didn't expect to be in a position where he'd have to make good on this promise, but Haynes kept the press cuttings and when Hill and the PFA had won their case he went to Trinder for his pay rise.

Trinder was good to his word, saying "Johnny Haynes is a top entertainer, and will be paid as one from now on. I will pay him £100 a week to play for Fulham." Bobby Robson thought that Trinder was sending out a message: "We've got the best player in the country, nobody's going to touch him, and we'll pay him whatever we have to."

All of this would have happened eventually, but Hill, as George Cohen put it, "seized the moment and accelerated the process quite dramatically. He was willing to put himself out."

Hill played between 1951 and 1961, an exciting time for the club. He was an energetic figure, charging back and forth and pushing his abilities to the limit. Tosh Chamberlain noted that "One thing you could count on with Jimmy

Hill was when the whistle blew, whether for the start of a game or simply for training, he'd run and run and never stop until the end. It makes me tired just thinking about him flying all over the place." Cohen added that "Hill was never more than a journeyman, but his redemption was that he knew it. He always tried to do the right thing on the field. He never tired of supporting team-mates when they had the ball, he never shirked a tackle and was always looking for a bit of free space."

LEFT & BELOW: The famous chin.

Haynes and Chairman Tommy Trinder. Trinder had made Haynes the highest paid player in the country.

1961–62 *Another Semi-final, slipping down the League*

1961–62 was about two things: a Cup run – Fulham reached the FA Cup semi-final – and an extraordinary 11-game losing streak that ran from the start of December to the end of February.

The losing streak came as something of a shock, as Fulham had made a decent start to the season. Six wins and five draws in the first 15 games suggested real progress, but Fulham lost their next three, beat Blackburn 2-0, then lost another 11.

In December Tommy Trinder applied for a bank loan to buy a new centre-forward, upsetting the National Union of Small Shopkeepers. Mr Thomas Lynch, Chairman of that organization, said: "A loan would be ridiculous. Small tradesmen are getting negligible loans for a legitimate purpose – the building up of a business. Why should a football club be allowed to borrow such a substantial sum? We are going to appeal to the Chancellor of the Exchequer not to loan money to football clubs until the credit squeeze is over."

Trinder, about to go on stage in Streatham, was curt in his response: "Mr Lynch has forgotten that a football club is a limited company. It is a business. It has shareholders, pays taxes and rates, employs people and has a colossal turnover. Let him take ninety two businesses in his union, compare them to the ninety two league clubs, and see who pays more to the government in the end."

In the end Trinder bought Jackie Henderson from Arsenal to play up front, but the signing made no difference to the team's form.

Johnny Haynes noted that the goal shortage was "Not bad luck. We're creating chances but just not getting them in." Bedford Jezzard added: "We will have some tactical practice matches on Thursday and Friday to try to overcome the problem. I'm sure the tide will turn this Saturday against Arsenal."

It didn't: Fulham lost 1-0.

Tommy Trinder was asked if the happy-go-lucky atmosphere at the club was contributing to the team's fortunes. "Probably," he replied. "It would be better if we were a bit more disciplined, but Fulham wouldn't be the same. If you crack the whip it's not going to make the boys play any better."

FA Cup quarter-final at home to Blackburn Rovers, March 1962.

But the Cup was a different story. Fulham beat Hartlepools, Walsall (after a replay) and then Port Vale, setting up a game against Blackburn in the quarter-finals.

Fulham had the better of an up-and-down game. After going behind, the Whites missed a penalty, equalized with an own goal, went behind again, then equalized again through Haynes. Despite the victory over Blackburn earlier in the season, Fulham had been strong underdogs before the game, so the draw was a good result.

In the replay Blackburn started well and Fulham's defence struggled to cope, but a goal from Maurice Cook, getting the better of three defenders, settled the game. Blackburn had a goal disallowed late on, but Fulham were through.

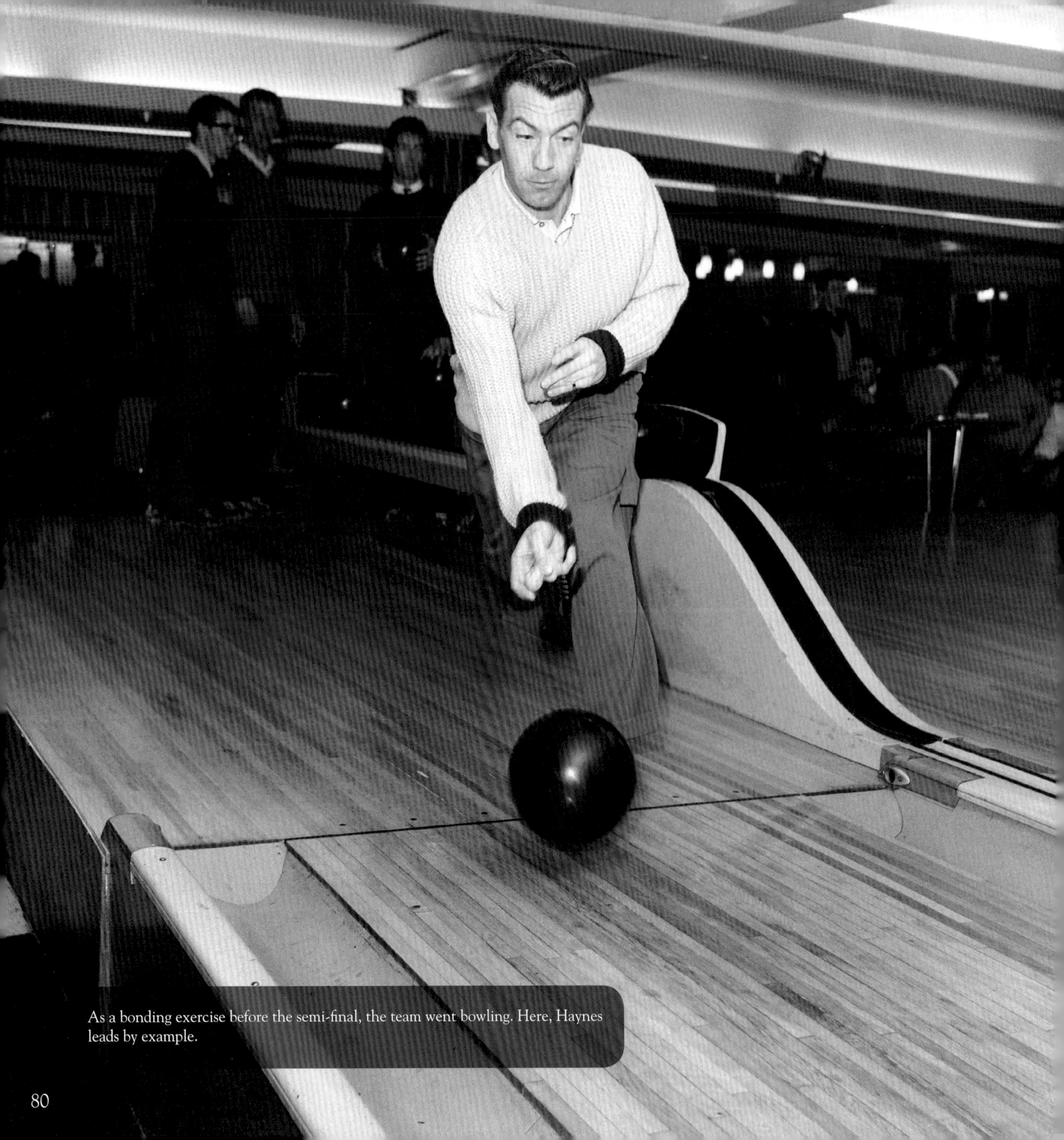

As a bonding exercise before the semi-final, the team went bowling. Here, Haynes leads by example.

Has Maurice Cook got the hang of it?

Fulham's FA Cup dreams were ended by top-of-the-table Burnley, but the Whites deserved so much more.

The first semi-final at Villa Park ended 1-1, but was controversial. Maurice Cook was taken down by Burnley keeper Adam Blacklaw in the 75th minute, a clear penalty. Referee Bill Clements waved play on. After the game all Clements would say is "the game is over. The decisions have been given." Cook's view: "It had to be a penalty. The ball was by him and I was on my way after it when he toppled me."

WOULD YOU HAVE GIVEN A PENALTY?

● Burnley 'keeper Blacklaw sticks out the foot which sends Fulham's goal-bound centre forward Cook stumbling into a penalty dispute at Villa Park.

Fulham robbed as Cook goes sprawling

By KEN JONES

Fulham 1, Burnley 1

FULHAM, the 12-1 Cup outsiders from Craven Cottage, were robbed of a penalty and the chance of a glittering, golden ride to Wembley in one tragic moment at Villa Park on Saturday.

Every Fulham footballer and fan screamed for a spot kick as centre forward hero Maurice Cook was sent sprawling by Burnley 'keeper Adam Blacklaw in the seventy-fifth minute.

And no one will ever change my view that West Bromwich referee *Bill Clements was cruelly wrong to* wave play on with a decision that put the breath back into battered Burnley.

All referee Clements would say was: "The game is over. The decisions have been given."

Cook, who had flipped the ball past a desperate, scrambling Blacklaw when he was crashed, told me afterwards:

"It had to be a penalty. The ball was by him and I was on my way after it when he toppled me.

Shocked

"I was flabbergasted when the *referee waved play on.* But what could you expect the way our luck went."

No one suffered more in this game than Cook.

For half an hour he ran Burnley and centre-half Tommy Cummings ragged. Two of his headers—both from gigantic Jimmy Langley throw-ins—flashed into the hands of Blacklaw, *who was lucky to rob* Cook of glory.

Burnley, battered by incessant Fulham attacks, looked on the way *to defeat when* Graham Leggat volleyed a twenty-sixth minute goal from a deadly Johnny Haynes pass.

Burnley, with McIlroy limping after the first ten minutes, managed to equalise through number one danger man right winger John Connelly in the fifty-first minute.

But it was Fulham, with Cook, Haynes and the hard running Henderson out on their own, who dominated.

Still their luck stayed away. Cook had a diving header beaten out by Blacklaw, and then Mullery had a power drive hooked away by Cummings with Blacklaw beaten.

Even after this I fancy Fulham to win the replay at Leicester next Monday night and make it an all-London Final on May 5.

Jimmy McIlroy will miss Burnley's League games against *Nottingham Forest* tomorrow and Wolves on Saturday in a bid to get fit for the replay.

Fulham had full backs Cohen and Langley injured, but both expect to be fit for Friday's game against Blackpool.

Cook had a stormer, and Burnley were on the back foot for much of the game. Graham Leggat volleyed Fulham ahead in the first half, Burnley nicked one back in the 51st minute, but try as they might, Fulham couldn't find a winner.

ABOVE: Fulham on the attack.

ABOVE: Macedo is beaten.

Macedo alert.

The replay saw more of the same. Burnley reshuffled their defence to better deal with Cook, but again found themselves taking a battering from an energetic Fulham side. Despite this, Burnley's Jimmy Robson scored twice, and Jimmy Langley's 88th-minute goal for Fulham was too late to make a difference. Johnny Haynes commented ruefully: "Well now they've all got their Spurs-Burnley final – but goodness knows how!"

Leggat goes close with an overhead kick.

Burnley score.

1962–63 *Haynes' Accident and Another Eventful Season*

In August 1962 Haynes was in another road accident, this time with more serious consequences. A red sports car driven by family friend June Max was involved in a crash on Blackpool promenade, and Haynes was seriously hurt.

He returned to action in the New Year for a 1-1 draw with Leyton Orient, played in a 3-1 win over Forest, then again in a 1-0 win over Ipswich. Then his knee flared up again. "Everything was going fine for half an hour," he said. "I was really enjoying the game. Then I went up to head the ball outside our penalty area and fell. I must have caught my foot in a divot as I fell, and my knee went." So he missed another two months, during which Fulham won another six games in a row (making eight in total), before finally losing at Burnley (4-0).

Haynes returned again for the season's last three games (Fulham lost them all), then had another operation to remove a cyst on the knee cartilage.

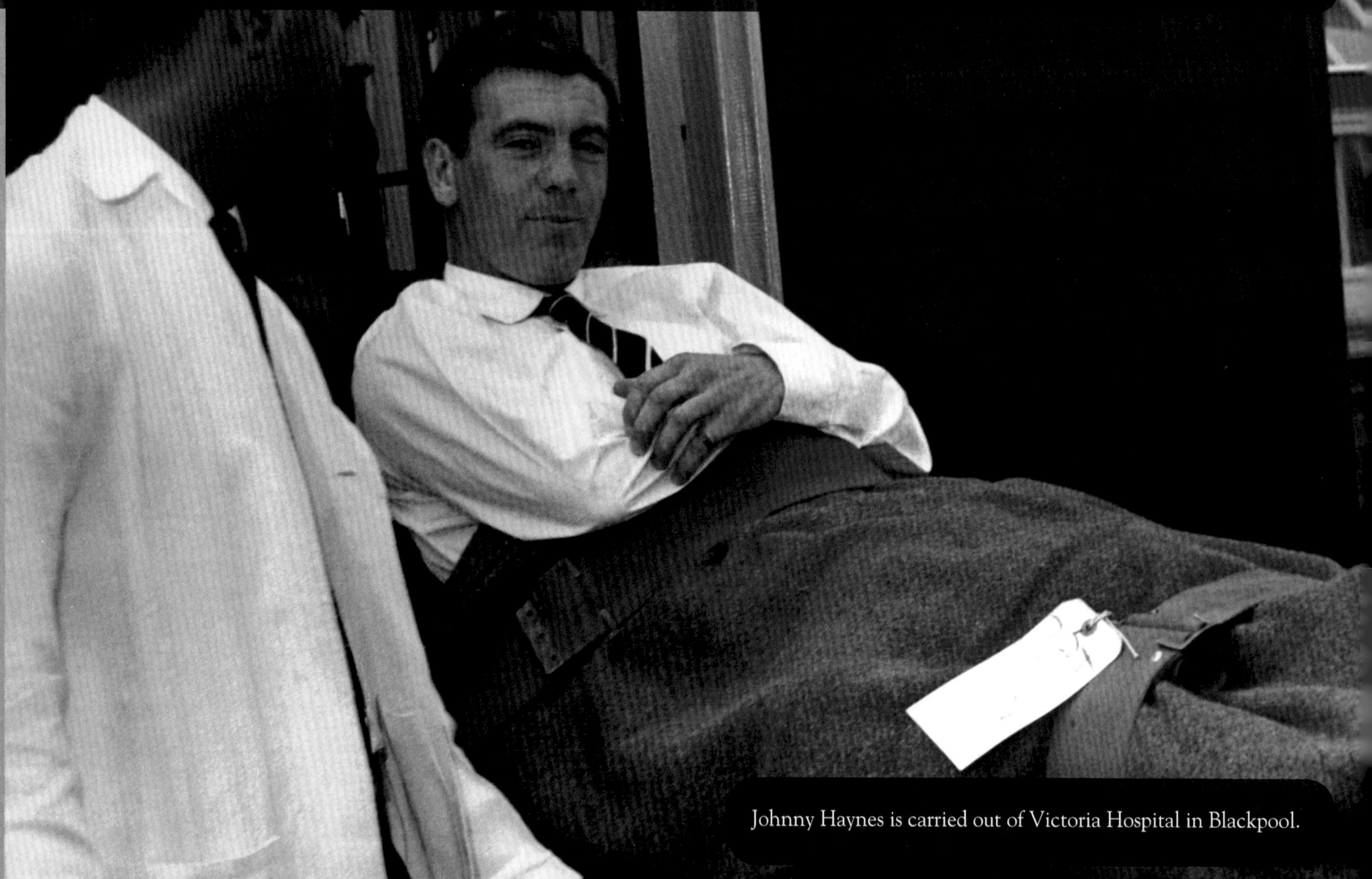

Johnny Haynes is carried out of Victoria Hospital in Blackpool.

On the mend: Haynes talks to Billy Wright, September 1962.

October 1962: the plaster is off.

Rehabilitation: Haynes with the reserves at Leatherhead.

The 1962–63 season started with the good news that Bobby Robson was coming back to Fulham. Just before the move, Robson noted that "I don't expect to reach an agreement which will keep me at the Hawthorns. After all, Fulham are prepared to pay me more than Albion, so I might just as well get to Craven Cottage and get to know the lads as soon as possible."

But two games into the season Robson picked up an injury away at Sheffield United, and the team were also soon without Johnny Haynes after the Blackpool car crash.

Fulham struggled. After a 1-0 defeat at Bolton the *Daily Mirror* said: "They had no forward capable of steering them, and with few midfield ideas – and fewer near goal – they looked a push-over."

Fulham surprised Everton the next time out, Stan Brown netting the only goal. "Everton came here thinking we were easy meat," said Bedford Jezzard.

Maybe so, but Everton might have had a point: next up Fulham were thrashed 6-1 by West Bromwich, losing Graham Leggat to a torn ankle ligament, an injury that would keep him out for six games.

And so it went. Fulham picked up results every so often, but in mid-February were 21st in the table, with only 16 points in 24 games.

Something had to change. Haynes returned to the side, which must have helped, but only lasted three games before the injury flared up again. Nevertheless, Fulham beat Nottingham Forest 3-1, their first home win for five months, with Robson in good form.

(John Key scored the third that day, and his return to the side is interesting. Key had only played five games prior to the Forest game, but his run in the team coincided with a bewildering run of eight wins in a row. Similarly, Pat O'Connell was brought back into the side for the Forest game, and also played every game in the winning streak.)

Fulham then beat Ipswich through a Leggat goal ("I couldn't really head the ball but I could see it all right on the ground," said a wounded Leggat), then after a win over Blackpool, beat Blackburn 1-0 despite losing Jackie Henderson to a broken leg after only 30 seconds.

All these injuries necessitated the selection of a 16-year-old Rodney Marsh for the next game against Villa, but Marsh it was who scored with a right-footed rocket on the hour to keep Fulham's run going.

Win number six came with a 3-2 win at Manchester City: Maurice Cook bagged two and O'Connell the other, and O'Connell scored again at Manchester United three days later in a 2-0 win. Fulham then beat West Ham 2-0 with goals from Cook and Key. A 4-0 defeat at traditional losing ground Burnley turned things around again, and Fulham only managed one win in the 10 remaining games after that.

It had been an extraordinary season, with injuries, bizarre shifts in form, and ultimately a respectable finishing position.

Craven Cottage, September 1962. Fulham lost 3-1 against Arsenal.

1963–64
A Relatively Ordinary Season

In 1963–64 Fulham consolidated their position as a good First Division side. The highlight was a 10-1 win over Ipswich Town on Boxing Day, in which Graham Leggat scored three goals in three minutes, the fastest ever hat-trick in the top division. Fulham lost to the same Ipswich side 4-2 two days later.

DAILY MIRROR, Friday, December 27, 1963 PAGE 19

'Fastest-ever' hat-trick by Leggat in fantastic Fulham win

TEN FOR THE 'TURKEYS'

"Allow me. . . ." Graham Leggat (right) picks up the ball for tired Ipswich 'keeper Roy Bailey after the third of the four goals he scored in Fulham's ten.

Picture (and the one on opposite page) by Mirror Sport cameraman Monte Fresco who went to Fulham after West Ham's morning match and thus saw twenty-onegoals scored in three hours of football.

By BILL HOLDEN: Fulham 10, Ipswich 1

TWO records crashed as Fulham's white whirlwind ripped through Ipswich. It was their best-ever win, and centre forward Graham Leggat achieved the fastest First Division hat-trick—his three goals came in a three-minute blitz that began in the seventeenth minute.

Leggat snatched a fourth goal in the last minute and this fantastic match produced a hat-trick, too, for left winger Bobby Howfield.

Manager Bedford Jezzard told me afterwards: "We had been playing just as well earlier this season, and not getting goals.

"It must have been all those lovely turkeys we gave *'em for Christmas that did it. From now on they get one every week."*

Ipswich chairman John Cobbold said: "What is an intelligent comment after this result? It could have gone either way—at least until the match began."

Fulham started their scoring spree in the fifteenth minute, when inside right Maurice Cook thumped in a centre from winger John Key.

Incredibly, Fulham might easily have been four goals up before that. It was so one-sided.

Once Cook had started the goal rush, it became another Klondike. Men made strikes, and others squandered chances prodigiously.

After Leggat's hat-trick, Howfield swerved a corner kick straight into the net *for No. 5 in the 42nd* minute.

Swerved

Gerry Baker, Ipswich centre forward, clipped the lead to 5—1 on the stroke of half-time.

Strangely, although the goals still came—Howfield (48 min.), left half Bobby Robson (83) and Howfield again (72), the crowd didn't rise to Fulham until two minutes from the end.

Then right half Alan Mullery made it 9—1 and suddenly the fans were jumping and roaring for that magical No. 10.

It came, with seconds to spare, from Leggat.

He hit a shot from 30 yards out on the wing which seemed magnetically *attracted inside the far up*right.

● *Fulham's previous best win? A 10—2 thrashing of Torquay on September 7, 1931.*

CONFIDENT CHARLTON STORM ON

By TOM LYONS

Swansea 1, Charlton 2

CHARLTON—methodical, confident, and always ready to snap up the half chance—are on their way back to the First Division on this form.

Inside left Dennis Edwards put Charlton ahead with an opportunist effort just after half-time.

Right winger Mike Kenning—later booked for arguing with a linesman—got the second from Eddie Firmani's pass after seventy-eight *minutes.* Inside right Derek Draper scored for Swansea in the last minute.

Massacre by the exiles of Chelsea

By MIRROR SPORT REPORTER

Blackpool 1, Chelsea 5

THIS was a massacre—and everybody could have gone home at half-time.

Chelsea, who had been exiled in a seaside hotel on Christmas Day, put out Blackpool's lights in the first forty-five minutes with swift and direct Soccer on a tricky pitch.

The rout began in the twentieth minute, Albert Murray scoring after 'keeper Tony Waiters had made three desperate clearances from the Chelsea twinklers.

Barry Bridges dived to head No. 2 after Frank Blunstone had gone through the defence.

Faster

Inside right Peter Houseman, deputising efficiently for Bobby Tambling, made it 3—0 in forty-one minutes.

Three minutes later the disconsolate Waiters, so often deserted by the men in front of him, dived a second late to a Bridges shot.

Blackpool made positional switches in the second half, but it made no difference.

Chelsea were always that yard faster to the ball.

Dave Durie pulled one back in the sixty-third minute, but Chelsea hit straight back through Terry Venables, who had spent most of the afternoon making goals for others.

All Chelsea had to lament was that full back Eddie McCreadie was "booked" by referee Arthur Luty.

EVEN THE HAMMERS' FANS HAD TO CHEER

West Ham 2, Blackburn 6

BLACKBURN, mud-caked and magnificent, squelched their way off the Upton Park pitch yesterday to a chorus of Cockney cheers, writes Harry Miller.

The League-leaders had given London another exhibition of their power . . . they have already hit Spurs for seven and Arsenal for four *this season.*

West Ham, who haven't won a League match since November 2, suffered their heaviest-ever home defeat.

Their tactics were all wrong, and their covering terrible. Blackburn, on a rain-lashed pudding of a pitch, banged the ball about with poise and precision. Hammers pressed on—to disaster—with a short-passing game.

Fred Pickering, a fiery, forceful centre forward, hit Blackburn's first goal after only five minutes.

Bryan Douglas — England must find room for him on this form—scored after thirty minutes. Andy McEvoy and Mike Ferguson took Blackburn's first half tally to four.

McEvoy completed a hat-trick with grand goals in the sixty-fifth and seventy-eighth minutes.

Pickering did the same by scoring again in the fifty-fifth and eighty-ninth minutes.

West Ham's woefully weak defence was wide open to every one of the goals.

Centre forward Johnny Byrne provided *the lone* crumb of West Ham comfort.

He scored in the tenth and fifty-ninth minutes and was *desperately* unlucky with a seventy-two minute thunderbolt that hit an upright.

PLAYBOY!

"I've got his autograph, but it isn't the name **YOU** called him when he missed that open goal!"

Mac stars—watched by Dad

By GERARD WALTER

Combined Services 9 pts., All Blacks 23

HAPPIEST man at Twickenham yesterday was the father of Mac Herewini, the All Blacks' star.

Fifty-year-old Maori McFarlane Herewini flew 12,000 miles from New Zealand to see his fly-half son against Wales last week-end only to find that Mac junior had been dropped.

But yesterday Mr. Herewini saw his son turn in a match-winning show as full back stand-in for Don Clarke.

Mac landed three penalty goals and converted a try in an All Blacks victory by a goal, three penalty goals and three tries to a try and two penalty goals

Deadly

And Mac's Dad said, "This has made my Christmas."

Combined Services couldn't match the tourists' *deadly finishing.*

The All Blacks' tries were scored by Bill Davies, Colin Meads, Ralph Caulton and Ian Macrae. For the Services, John Brown went over and John MacDonald got the penalty goals.

GALE STOPS PLAY

Gale-force winds held up play in the match between the South African cricket *tourists and* a Tasmanian combined team in Hobart yesterday. The bails kept falling off.

Jack Potter, 25-year-old Victorian, hit 123 not out in the combined side's first innings score of 218. The tourists hit 33 without loss.

EMERSON'S WIN BOOSTS AUSSIES

Roy Emerson beat Wimbledon champion Chuck McKinley to put Australia, the holders, level at 1—1 with America in the Davis Cup challenge round in Adelaide yesterday.

Emerson won 6—3, 3—6, 7—5, 7—5 after Denis Ralston had beaten John Newcombe 6—4, 6—1, 3—6, 4—6, 7—5.

KING KEEPS THEM IN THE HUNT

Colchester 2, Reading 1

READING made Colchester fight all the way for a win that keeps them in the promotion hunt.

It was not until the 75th minute that Martyn King scored the winning goal.

Reading had snatched a surprise lead in the 49th minute, when full back Gordon Neat scored from a Johnny Walker free-kick.

For a spell Colchester looked bound for defeat, but a snap goal by Bobby Hunt after fifty-six minutes put them back in the game.

SPORTS SUMMARY

ATHLETICS

BATTERSEA PARK. — 3½-mile Road Walk: R. Hall (Bexley, allowance 1m. 50s.) bt E. Hall (Lancs, scratch) by 50 yards. 120 Yards: D. Rees (Tooting), 12.5s. 2 Miles: J. Hilton (Fulham) 8m. 57s. Shot: O. Ryan (Surrey) 39ft. 6½in.

CRICKET

SHEFFIELD SHIELD (Melbourne).—New South Wales (1st innings): 326 for eight (B Simpson 135) v. Victoria.

HOBART, TASMANIA. — Combined Eleven: 218 (J. Potter 133 not) South Africans: 33 for no wkt.

LAWN TENNIS

DAVIS CUP CHALLENGE ROUND (Adelaide). — Australia (holders) 1, America 1. D. Ralston (U S) bt J. Newcombe (A) 6—4, 6—1, 3—6, 4—6, 7—5; R. Emerson (A) bt C. McKinley (U S) 6—3, 3—6, 7—5, 7—5.

RUGBY UNION

TOUR MATCH.—Combined Services 9 pts., New Zealanders 23

CLUB MATCHES. — Wasps 3, Metro Police 5; Bath 24, O. Blues 3; Bedford 33, O. Paulines 3; Cardiff 24, Welsh Acads 3; Coventry 26, Cheltenham 3; Gloucester 18, O M T 0; Leicester 8, Barbarians 13; Liverpool 12, Waterloo 0; Llanelly 3, London Welsh 13; Maesteg 0, Bridgend 3; Moseley 3, O. Edwardians 3; Neath 6, Aberavon 3; Newport 25, Watsonians 11; Northampton 16, Penarth 16; Nuneaton 11, Rugby 3; Pontypool 6, Pontypridd 0; Redruth 3, Camborne 9; Swansea 16; Univ. Ath. Union 3; Torquay 19, Teignmouth 0; Weston-super-Mare 5, Clifton 0; Edinburgh Acads 0, London Scottish 9

MOTOR RACING

BRANDS HATCH. — Unlimited Single-Seater Racing Cars (25 laps): 1, A. V. Hegbourne (Cooper-Ford) 22m. 56.2s., 64.87 m.p.h. 2, J Mastin (Lotus-Ford); 3, M Long (Lotus-Ford). Fastest lap: Hegbourne and Mastin (1m. 6.4s., 67.23 m.p.h.). Grand Touring Cars over 1,600 c.c. (10 laps): 1, J. Dean (Jaguar E-type) (11m. 19.6s., 66.27 m.p.h.); 2, K. Baker (Jaguar E-type); 3, J. R. Stoop (Porsche Carrera). Fastest Lap: Stoop (68.58 m.p.h.)

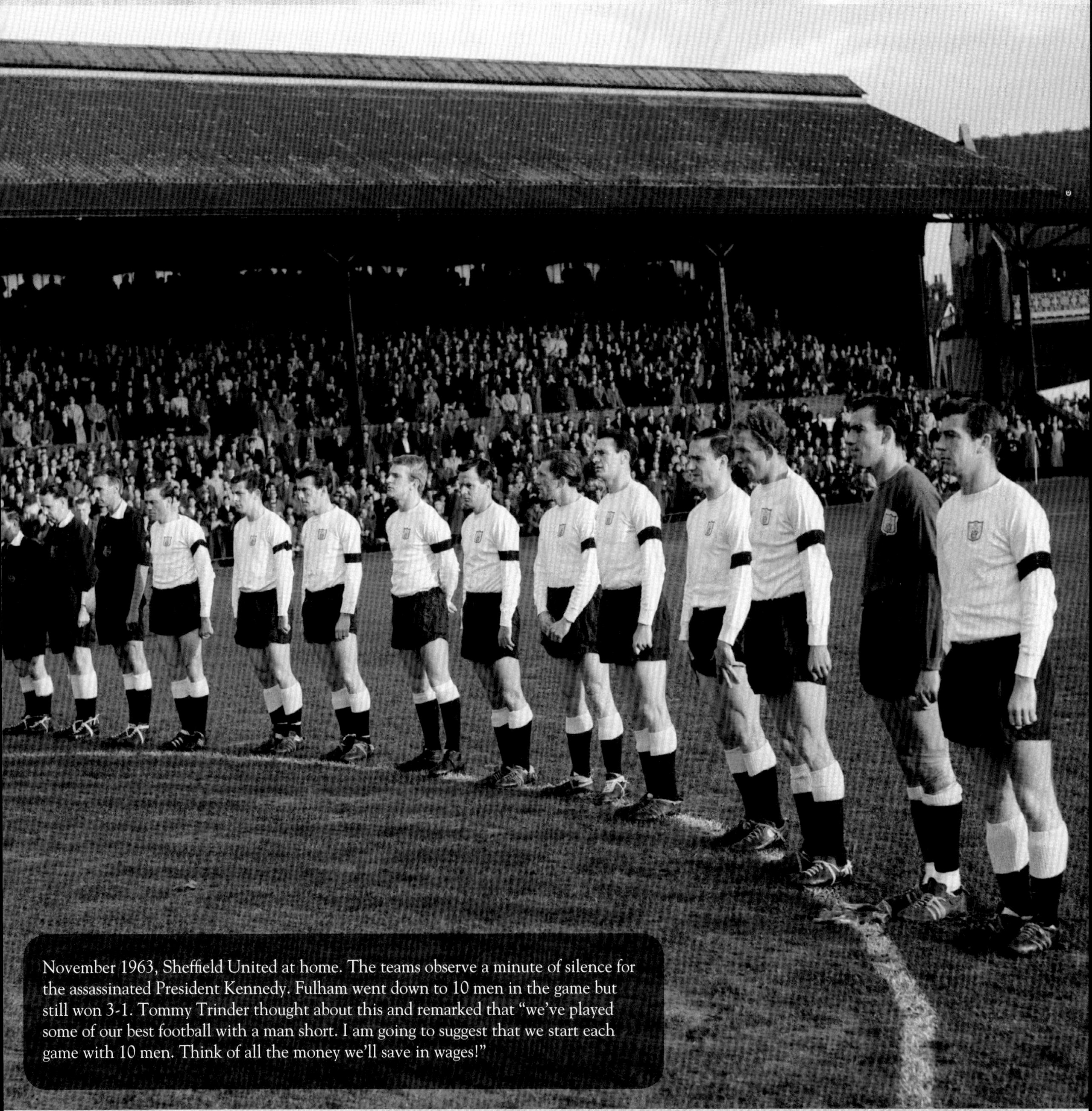

November 1963, Sheffield United at home. The teams observe a minute of silence for the assassinated President Kennedy. Fulham went down to 10 men in the game but still won 3-1. Tommy Trinder thought about this and remarked that "we've played some of our best football with a man short. I am going to suggest that we start each game with 10 men. Think of all the money we'll save in wages!"

FOOTBALL
–STATS–

Tosh Chamberlain

Name: Tosh Chamberlain

Born: London 1934

Position: Forward

Fulham playing career: 1954–1965

Club appearances: 204

Goals: 64

–LEGENDS–

Tosh Chamberlain

Robin Lawler, Fulham's Irish left-back, had a gift for nicknames. Johnny Haynes became "the little nark" (Narky for short), on account of his stroppy on-field behaviour. Bedford Jezzard was "Pud", Arthur Stevens "Pablo", and Trevor Chamberlain became "Tosh".

Chamberlain was a great friend of Johnny Haynes, the pair having played representative football together as schoolboys, and Chamberlain was influential in Haynes coming to Fulham in the first place. But on the field their relationship was frequently strained. Alan Mullery tells of how, at his first game at the Cottage, he saw Chamberlain withdraw from the action to have a cigarette in the stand. Haynes pinged a 50-yard pass to where Chamberlain would have been, and got very angry. Chamberlain shouted back "When I'm out here waiting, you never pass to me. Then when I'm having a fag, you give me the ball!" The Haynes–Chamberlain rows happened, George Cohen reckoned, about once a match.

There are dozens of funny Tosh Chamberlain stories, and certainly he played his part in what was a very colourful Fulham side. There is perhaps a danger that the comedy overshadows the player, and while Chamberlain wasn't in the same league as some of his team-mates, he was a more than decent performer: his 64 goals in 204 games is a more than useful record.

Chamberlain had a tremendously powerful shot, to the extent that he was called Trevor "The Shot" Chamberlain in a 1959 newspaper article. His critics would argue that these shots didn't always go where they were meant to, and there is truth to that, but he was nevertheless capable of flashes of brilliance. On Boxing Day 1956, for example, Fulham had lost three straight and were playing a Blackburn side that had won six in a row. Fulham, with typical contrariness, won 7-2, and Chamberlain scored a hat-trick, the first of which saw him collect the ball from goalkeeper Ian Black, run the length of the pitch, then blast the ball over the opposing goalkeeper.

He'd scored another hat-trick the season before against Doncaster. Having already scored twice, Fulham were awarded a penalty. Chamberlain took it and scored, but goalkeeper Joe Gregg made no attempt to save it, throwing his cap down in disgust. "The referee told me Haynes would take it," he said. "When Chamberlain ran up I didn't know what was happening." Chamberlain protested: "Johnny told me to have a go to try to get my hat-trick." He had to re-take it, but scored again.

4th May 1963: half-back Eddie Lowe looks around before his last Fulham game. Lowe amassed 511 Fulham appearances between 1950 and 1963, a record not broken until Johnny Haynes came along.

Tommy Trinder meets Frank Osborne, supposedly to discuss a Spurs offer for Johnny Haynes, August 1964.

1964–65 *There May Be Trouble Ahead…*

Things started to go wrong in 1964. Tommy Trinder made some comments in the *Daily Mail* that weren't especially positive about his team, and had incorporated Fulham into his popular comedy act. The players were furious. One said "We are seething, and have been for some weeks, about Trinder's stage act down in Margate. He has been ridiculing the club and the players."

Jimmy Hill led the revolt, confronting Trinder over the comments and also asking where Fulham's money was going. Alan Mullery had been sold to Spurs, Johnny Haynes was keen to follow (the club said no), and Tony Macedo said that if Haynes was going so was he. George Cohen had been unhappy about his contract for a while, and did get a new one, but Graham Leggat did not, and asked for a transfer.

Bedford Jezzard was asked about the negativity at Fulham: "I have a job to do and I am going to do it. I don't care what anyone is supposed to have said," but this masked a deep unhappiness at the way the club was being run. Mullery had been sold over his head, and indeed he found out about the transfer from Haynes in the dressing room during a game. Jezzard stormed straight up to the board room. It was "just business," he was told.

DAILY MIRROR, Saturday, August 29, 1964 PAGE 19

CRISIS COTTAGE

By BILL HOLDEN

FULHAM, the crisis club of Soccer, torn by back-stage strife, were sure of one thing last night: whatever happens the game WILL go on.

They tackle West Bromwich Albion at the Hawthorns this afternoon. And despite their anger at comments alleged to have been made by chairman Tommy Trinder the players have dedicated themselves to 100 per cent.-plus effort for success.

They will be without skipper and former England star JOHNNY HAYNES, one of the central figures in the Craven Cottage crisis.

Haynes has a knee injury—the same knee that kept him out of Soccer for nearly six months after his car crash at Blackpool two years ago.

His place at inside left today goes to young Stan Brown. That means Fulham have overlooked fit and willing-to-play Scottish international GRAHAM LEGGAT, who added to the club's troubles this week when he asked for a transfer.

Near the end of last season Fulham, who have never won a major honour, sold England wing-half star ALAN MULLERY to Spurs for £75,000.

Just before this season began Haynes dropped a bombshell by saying he wanted to join Spurs if they bid for him.

Emergency

Then Young England goalkeeper TONY MACEDO announced that if Fulham let Haynes go he, too, would ask for a move.

After an emergency board meeting, Fulham told Haynes he would not be released.

He agreed with the verdict and Fulham's troubles seemed to be over when their England full back, GEORGE COHEN, who had been in dispute over wage terms, finally signed a full contract.

But it all flared up again this week when Leggat asked for a move.

Upset

The Fulham fans are rapidly losing patience with the club over these internal squabbles.

They slow handclapped as Fulham lost their opening match at home to West Ham last Saturday. Some of them shouted to the director's, demanding new players should be bought.

Other fans have decided to boycott the club until they do buy new players. There have also been calls for changes on the board.

Fulham HAVE tried to buy new players. "So far they have failed," general manager FRANK OSBORNE told me.

He refused to comment on the sensational players' meeting yesterday which followed the remarks chairman Trinder is alleged to have made.

Team manager BEDFORD JEZZARD was also silent. But he gave the feeling of the whole club when he said:

"I have a job to do—and I am going to go on doing it. I don't care what anyone is supposed to have said."

But the players say: We'll win today

The crowd on match day at Craven Cottage . . . home of Fulham Football Club.

STAN BROWN

PLAYBOY!

Ah! They never forget a face here—he flagged their centre forward offside a coupla seasons ago!"

WORLD FIGHT FOR HOWARD—AFTER A FILM

By TOM LYONS

HOWARD WINSTONE, British and European featherweight champion, can have his long-delayed world title chance against champion Sugar Ramos, Mexican-based Cuban, at Wembley on November 24.

World champion Ramos has agreed with promoter Jack Solomons to defend his crown against Winstone.

The Welshman will make up his mind after he and his manager, Eddie Thomas, have seen a film of the recent Ramos-Floyd Robertson world title bout at a private showing in London on Tuesday.

Neither Eddie nor Winstone have seen Ramos box as a featherweight. When they saw him demolish Sammy McSpadden last year he was 9lb. over the featherweight limit.

Yesterday a delighted Winstone told me: "Ramos is certainly a class fighter, but I am very confident."

The world title clash will cut across Winstone's defence of his European title against French champion Yves Demarets.

First

But manager Thomas said last night: "A world title match takes precedence over a European championship bout."

The Ramos-Winstone fight is the second "leg" of Solomons's autumn treble. He stages the world welterweight title fight between the holder, Emile Griffith, and Welshman Brian Curvis, at Wembley on September 22, and hopes to get lightweight champion Dave Charnley a world title shot against Carlos Ortiz before the end of the year.

WBA BAN CLAY-LISTON RETURN FIGHT

THE World Boxing Association of the United States yesterday unanimously refused to sanction the planned return world heavyweight title fight between Cassius Clay and ex-champion Sonny Liston.

The WBA's opposition was based mainly on its claim that promotional rights for the return were assigned to Intercontinental Promotions even before the first Clay-Liston fight last February.

This violated their ban on return-bout contracts.

Teddy Waltham, secretary of the British Boxing Board of Control, said it was "great news."

"We have always taken a strong stand against this particular fight and have written to the WBA that it should not take place."

Pamela is golf champion

PAMELA TREDINNICK, 18, is the new British girl golf champion.

In yesterday's final at Camberley Heath, Surrey, she defeated Kathleen Cumming, 17-year-old bank clerk from Tayport, Fife, by 2 and 1.

In her semi-final, Pamela (West Sussex) toppled the favourite, Shirley Ward (Princes), who had beaten her to win the English girls' title a fortnight previously.

Victory against Shirley came at the nineteenth hole after a tense four-hour duel, and Pamela went on to shatter Miss Cumming's hopes of becoming the first Scot to win the championship since 1915.

Pamela was three up at the turn, but Kathleen pulled back to only one down at the fourteenth.

A birdie three at the fifteenth after a chip into the cup put Pamela in sight of victory and she clinched it with a par four at the seventeenth.

SUMMARY

LAWN TENNIS

BUDLEIGH SALTERTON CHAMPIONSHIPS.—Men's singles, semi-finals: M. Cox bt C. Iles 6—0, 6—4; C. Applewhaite bt G. C. Bluett 4—6, 16—14, 6—2. Women's singles, semi-finals: P. Toyne (Australia) bt H. Allen 6—4, 8—2; Mrs. J. A. G. Lloyd bt N. Truman 1—6, 7—5, 7—5.

BOWLS

ENGLISH WOMEN'S CHAMPIONSHIPS (Wimbledon Park, Surrey).—Pairs final: M. Steele, Mrs. V. Stevens (Watling Association Middx) bt Mrs. I. Kelly, Mrs. W. Hollow (Newton Abbott) 21—10. Singles final: Mrs. D. Dowling (W. Streatham) bt Mrs. J. Lucking (Royal Household, Berks) 22—20. Rinks final: Sarton House, Lincs. bt Broadway, Worcs. 16—14.

Pools Check

FIRST DIVISION (3.0)

Arsenal v. A. Villa
Birmingham v. Stoke (3.15)
Blackburn v. Liverpool
Blackpool v. Sheff. Wed.
Chelsea v. Sunderland
Everton v. Tottenham
Leeds v. Wolverhampton
Leicester v. Man. Utd.
Sheff. Utd. v. Burnley
W B A v. Fulham

SECOND DIVISION (3.0)

Bolton v. Coventry
Derby v. Bury
Ipswich v. Preston
Manchester C. v. Northampton
Middlesbrough v. Huddersfield
Newcastle v. Southampton
Plymouth v. Cardiff (3.15)
Portsmouth v. Charlton
Rotherham v. Norwich
Swansea v. C. Palace (3.15)
Swindon v. Leyton Orient

THIRD DIVISION (3.0)

Bristol City v. Walsall
Gillingham v. Watford
Grimsby v. Exeter
Hull v. Workington
Luton v. Bristol Rov.
Mansfield v. Oldham
Peterborough v. Bournemouth
Port Vale v. Colchester (3.15)
Reading v. Southend
Shrewsbury v. Barnsley (3.15)

FOURTH DIVISION (3.0)

Barrow v. Oxford Utd.
Bradford C. v. Stockport (6.30)
Chester v. Torquay (3.15)
Chesterfield v. Bradford (6.30)
Crewe v. Darlington
Doncaster v. Aldershot
Halifax v. Wrexham
Hartlepools v. Brighton
Millwall v. York (3.15)
Newport v. Tranmere (3.15)
Notts Co. v. Southport
Rochdale v. Lincoln

SCOTTISH LEAGUE CUP (3.0)

Aberdeen v. St. Mirren
Airdrie v. Hibernian
Alloa v. Stirling
Arbroath v. Queen's Park
Clyde v. Albion
Cowdenbeath v. Brechin
Dumbarton v. Ayr
Dundee Utd. v. Motherwell
Falkirk v. Dundee
Hamilton v. E. S Clydebank
Hearts v. Partick Thistle
Kilmarnock v. Celtic
Montrose v. East Fife
Morton v. Berwick
Raith v. Queen of South
Rangers v. St. Johnstone
Stranraer v. Stenhousemuir
Third Lanark v. Dunfermline

OLDHAM GET MAR[T…] FOR £12,000

Blackpool full back B[…] Martin, who has [been] Jimmy Armfield's pa[rtner] for the last five sea[sons] was transferred to Ol[dham] Athletic last night at [a fee] of around £12,000. Ma[rtin], 28, who has been o[n the] transfer list since th[e end] of last season, was s[igned] from a local youth [club] twelve years ago.

DAWSON IS UN[…]

Swindon right back [...] Dawson has a sl[ight] injury and misses [...] home game against [Leyton] Orient. Terry W[...] deputises.

CINEMAS

ASTORIA, Char. X-rd. Ger. 5385. Samuel Bronston's THE FALL OF THE ROMAN EMPIRE (U). Sep. perfs. 2.30 & 7.30. Sunday at 6.30. DOMINION, Tot. Ct.-rd. (Mus. 2176) CLEOPATRA (A) in Todd-AO. Mats Daily at 2.0. Evngs. at 7.0. Sunday 4.0. All bookable at Th. & Agents.

EXHIBITIONS

ADVERTISEMENT

Daily Mirror

Fulham players accuse comedian-chairman

SOCCER CLUB REVOLT AGAINST TRINDER

3d. Saturday, August 29, 1964 No. 18,877

The day a golf club's hunters shot a No 4 iron

WHAT a rotten round! Golfer Terry Wilkins was so disgusted with his efforts that he tossed up his No. 4 iron.

It soared into the air—and landed on the topmost branch of a 100ft. elm tree.

There it stayed. Stuck. And it took three blasts from a shotgun yesterday to get it down again....

Terry let fly with the iron on the fairway of the Gainsborough Golf Club in Lincolnshire a week ago.

Threw

Club members threw sticks and stones to the top of the tree.

Former club captain Alan Williamson shinned up a nearby 80 foot elm.

He tried to dislodge the iron with a pole.

Club captain Dr. William Ward suggested fetching the fire brigade.

Then Mr. Williamson, a garage proprietor, took his gun to the course and fired three shots.

He was reloading for a fourth when the No. 4 iron finally dropped.

Last night the three spent cartridge cases were on view in a showcase at the clubhouse.

Match

Said Dr. Ward: "They will be preserved to commemorate an exceptional golfing-shooting performance."

Student Malcolm Bell, 21, was one of Terry's opponents in the match.

He said: "Terry played a bad shot to the green. He yelled 'Dash'—or words to that effect—then slung his club into the tree."

Mrs. Looney . . . "Perfume behind the ears."

By KEN JONES and BRIAN McCONNELL

A BIG Soccer row blew up yesterday when Fulham players accused their club chairman, comedian Tommy Trinder, of "jibes" at their expense.

The players, including £100-a week captain Johnny Haynes, held a grandstand meeting at the Craven Cottage ground, London, at which they voiced angry protests over statements attributed to Mr. Trinder.

'Resented'

After the seventy-minute meeting, the players issued a statement which said:

"Statements by the chairman of Fulham Football Club on the radio and in the Press, and presumably with the knowledge and consent of the directors, are deeply resented by the players.

Such irresponsible statements have an unsetting effect on team spirit and they make the job of our team manager Bedford Jezzard, in whom we have complete confidence, that much harder.

It would be appreciated by the players if jibes at our expense would cease.

We feel certain that we would then be able to give the club and the public our wholehearted endeavour."

Tommy Trinder (right) with Fulham manager Frank Osborne.

Protest at 'jibes'

The Fulham players called their meeting yesterday after a Daily Mail article in which Trinder criticised individual players and members of Fulham's staff.

'Trouble'

Their decision to issue a statement was passed on to general manager Frank Osborne, who said last night:

"They told me what they had decided to do and I left it to them. We have had enough trouble lately. I have no comment to make about it."

One player said: "If the Fulham club have no ambitions, we certainly have. We don't want to be associated with the music hall—we want to be associated with a football club."

Another said: "We are seething, and have been for some weeks, about Trinder's stage act down at Margate. He has been ridiculing the club and the players."

The player added: "It's a good thing that Mr. Trinder has a job down at Margate and can't get to our game at West Bromwich tomorrow.

"There would have been an almighty row on the train if he had been coming with us."

Fulham director Jack Walsh said last night: "It is a difficult situation. Nothing definite has been arranged by us as directors to deal with the situation.

"I have not been in touch with Mr. Trinder, and he has not been in touch with me. His professional affairs can make it difficult for him to attend a meeting."

'Unfair'

Last night at the Lido, Cliftonville, where Tommy Trinder is appearing, newspapermen were told: "Mr. Trinder does not want to see anybody, and doesn't want to comment."

Mr. Cliff Lloyd, secretary of the Professional Footballers' Association, said last night:

"I am absolutely staggered that such a responsible official as Mr. Trinder has apparently criticised his players in this way. I think it is quite extraordinary and unfair."

CRISIS AT CRAVEN COTTAGE

—See Page Nineteen.

IT'S CONSPIRACY, SAYS KISS-CASE MAN

THE man who is being sued by widow Mrs. Catherine Looney over an alleged "kiss and cuddle" claimed yesterday it was all a conspiracy.

The man, 45-year-old Gaylord Richards, says that it was Mrs. Looney's perfume that made him kiss her.

And his counsel told a court in Los Angeles that other women in the office where Mrs. Looney works persuaded her to dab perfume behind her ears—and Richards fell for it.

Name of the perfume? "To a Wild Rose."

Other workers at the firm, where Richards works as a security guard, said that 33-year-old Mrs. Looney did not discourage him.

Lawyer Joseph Spray, for the firm, said that what Richards did was not within the scope of his employment.

Mrs. Looney is claiming £12,000 damages. The case will be heard by a jury.

Gaylord Richards

In early December that year, following a poor run of results, Jezzard resigned. Speaking from his pub in Hammersmith, he said: "You won't get anything from me on this. I suggest you talk to the Chairman. I have got nothing to say." Two days later he was more forthcoming, allowing that he had resigned in November, and that he simply wanted to work in his pub for a while. Bedford Jezzard's time at Fulham was over.

Vic Buckingham replaced him, and tried to toughen the club up. There remains a suspicion that he tried to do too much, too soon. He was prepared to pick fights with whomsoever he felt needed a kick up the backside, including Johnny Haynes, who was at one point dropped for lack of effort. Buckingham moved on players like Cook, Langley, Keetch and Leggat, but (as per Jezzard), hadn't had the money to bring in quality replacements.

New manager Vic Buckingham watches his team training.

The team continued to struggle. Here we see Fulham visiting Stoke City, a 3-1 defeat (right). Sir Stanley Matthews and Jimmy Langley go head-to-head, 86 years old between them (below).

5

Fulham FC, August 1965. Left to right, back row: Cohen, Dempsey, Keetch, Macedo, McClelland, Mealand, Callaghan, Robson; Middle row: Key, Brown, Leggat, Haynes, Marsh, O'Connell; Front row: Pearson and Dyson.

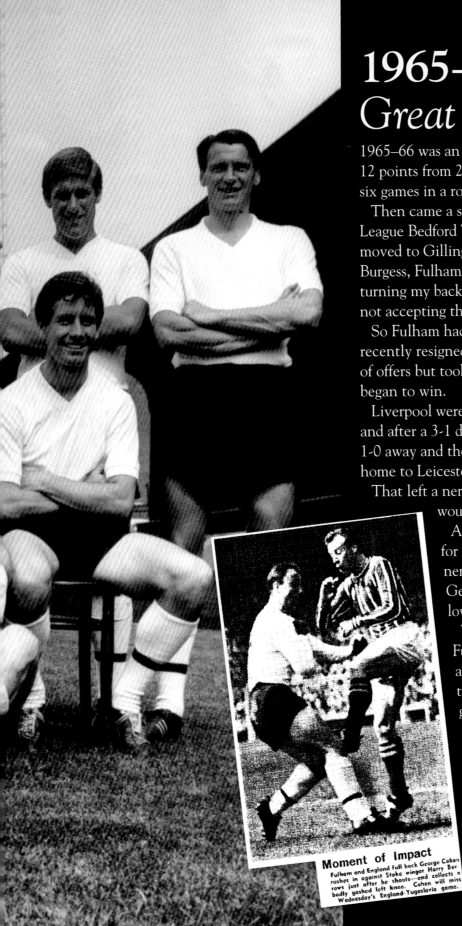

1965–66 *The Original Great Escape*

1965–66 was an extraordinary season. At the end of 1965 Fulham had 12 points from 23 games and were bottom of the table. They had lost six games in a row.

Then came a sequence of events that saved the season. Southern League Bedford Town lost their manager, Basil Hayward, who had moved to Gillingham. Bedford offered Hayward's old job to Ron Burgess, Fulham's coach. Burgess accepted. "I've got regrets about turning my back on Fulham," said Burgess, "but I would have regretted not accepting the chance to take over Bedford even more."

So Fulham had a job to fill, and offered it to Dave Sexton, who had recently resigned as manager of Leyton Orient. Sexton had a number of offers but took the Fulham job, and almost immediately, Fulham began to win.

Liverpool were beaten 2-0, Villa 5-2, Sunderland 3-0, WBA 2-1, and after a 3-1 defeat at home to Leeds, Fulham beat the same team 1-0 away and then defeated Sheffield Wednesday 4-2. They lost 4-0 at home to Leicester, but beat Northampton 4-2 and Forest 2-1.

That left a nerve-wracking finale against Stoke City, in which a point would probably be enough to ensure survival.

Moment of Impact

Fulham and England full back George Cohen rushes in against Stoke winger Harry Burrows just after he shoots—and collects a badly gashed left knee. Cohen will miss Wednesday's England-Yugoslavia game.

After 10 minutes George Cohen was stretchered off, and for much of the first half Fulham's play was nervous and disjointed. Stoke scored when Gerry Bridgwood beat McClelland with a low cross-shot.

FIRST DIVISION

Nottm. For. .. 1 Fulham 2

Bottom Positions

SECOND DIVISION

Charlton .... 2 Coventry 0

THIRD DIVISION

Bournemouth .. 0 Brentford 1

Swindon ..... 0 Shrewsbury 0

Watford .... 2 Scunthorpe 1

Workington .... 0 Bristol R. 0

FOURTH DIVISION

Barnsley ...... 0 Lincoln 1

Rochdale .... 3 Hartlepools 1

The game became extraordinarily tense as Fulham's desperation grew. A good penalty appeal was refused, but Fulham's luck turned with eight minutes left. The Stoke goalkeeper was fouled by Allan Clarke as he came for a corner and dropped the ball, Les Barrett's shot was headed off the line, John Dempsey had a go – also blocked – then Clarke finally pounced from close by, smashing home the goal that kept Fulham up.

At the end of the season Sexton left to be chief coach at Arsenal. Fulham missed him.

After Tony Macedo broke his jaw at Northampton, reserve goalkeeper Jack McClelland took over in goal. His first four games were all defeats, but after briefly losing his place when Macedo returned, McClelland played from February onwards, a key player in Fulham's miraculous escape. Macedo was having some personal issues, and at one point demanded to leave Fulham. He complained about the transfer fee Fulham were asking for, then considered that he would rather leave football altogether than stay (he had a job offer outside the game). He returned and had an excellent season in 1966–67, but then left to play for Colchester.

Here McClelland saves well against Arsenal in a 1-0 win on New Year's Day 1966.

LEVI'S

The winning run that saved Fulham's season started on 26th February. Two Steve Earle goals beat Champions elect, Liverpool.

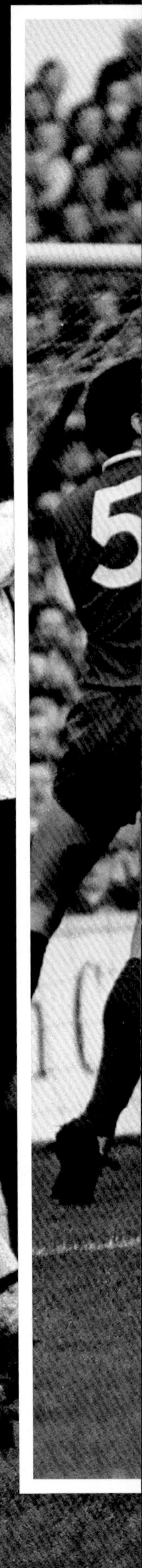

Leggat challenges against Liverpool.

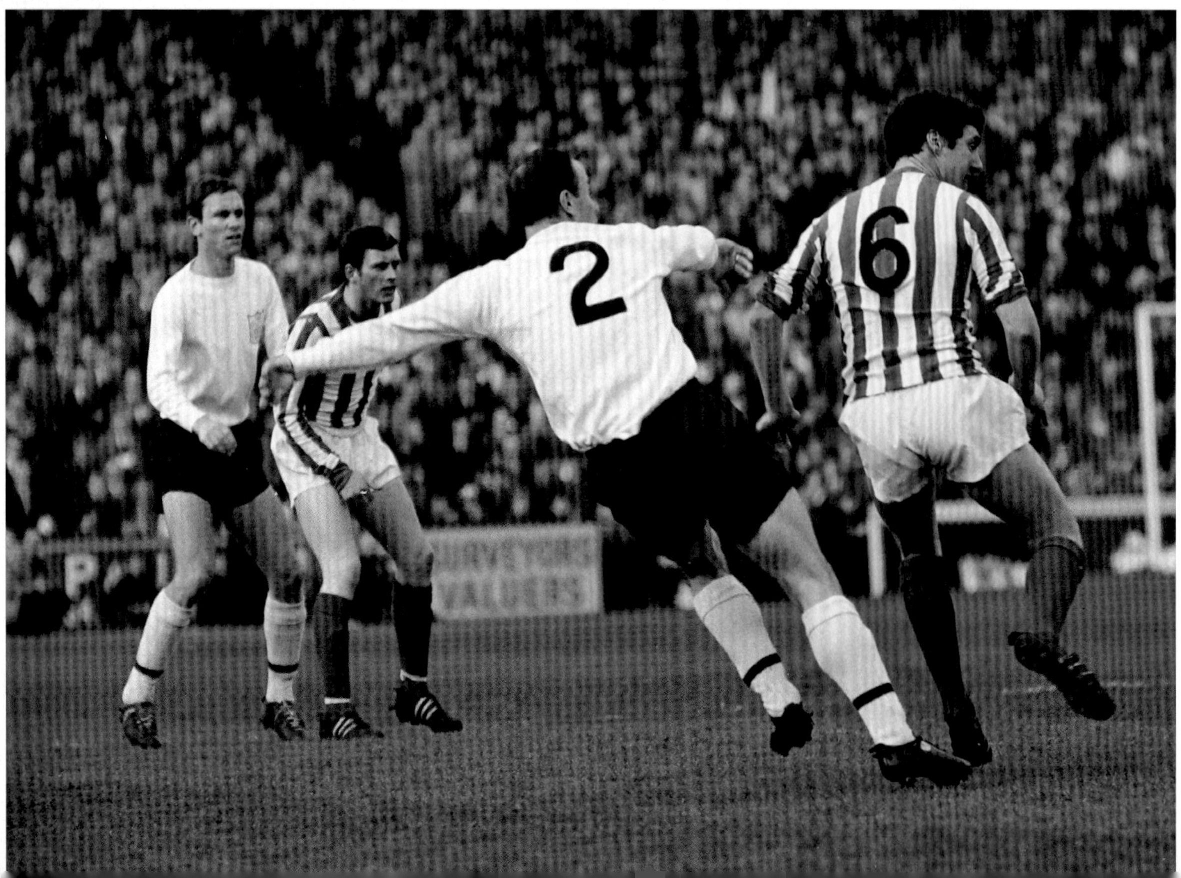

ABOVE: After beating Aston Villa 5-2 at Villa Park, Sunderland came to the Cottage. Fulham won 3-0, Leggat scoring twice. The other, shown here, came from a Hurley own goal.

LEFT: George Cohen clears the danger.

LHAM HIGH ST.
DRINK
BEER

Fulham beat West Bromwich Albion 2-1 at the start of April. Haynes scored both goals.

McClelland flies high, punches clear.

Tension: Fulham need an equalizer in the season's penultimate game against Stoke City.

With eight minutes left, and following the mother of all goal-mouth scrambles, Allan Clarke slams home his first goal for Fulham. It kept his team in the First Division.

Celebration!

FULHAM

–LEGENDS–

George Cohen

Described in Maurice Golesworthy's 1964 *Soccer Who's Who* as "cool as an iceberg while under pressure this full-back has blossomed into one of the most dependable defenders in the Football League. An unobtrusive player who turns in valuable performances game after game without attracting the glare of publicity."

This seems about right. Cohen was a fantastic servant of Fulham, and after making his debut in 1956, went on to play regularly until 1967, when he picked up a knee injury that eventually ended his career. His last game was in 1969, when he was only 30. Cohen, a remarkably fit man, would surely have had a few more years in him from there, and would probably have played an important role for England in the 1970 World Cup.

Cohen was a model professional, the sort of player that would improve every team. He was famous for his overlapping style of play: whether the ball found him on the flank or not, his runs would force defences to cover him, opening up space for others. His fitness and speed ensured that he was able to recover his own defensive position after these surges. His concentration was second to none.

Cohen, of course, was a key member of Sir Alf Ramsey's 1966 World Cup winning side.

FOOTBALL
–STATS–

George Cohen

Name: George Cohen

Born: London 1939

Position: Right-back

Fulham playing career: 1956–1969

Club appearances: 459

Goals: 6

England appearances: 37

Goals: 0

1966–67 A *Temporary Respite*

This being mid-sixties Fulham, nothing was straightforward. Vic Buckingham's side for the day did not include Johnny Haynes. "I have picked a side to do a job," said Buckingham. "Johnny came to see me and was upset. One expected that, and I can understand why. But I am happy with the side I picked, and there is definitely a future for Johnny at Fulham."

Fulham lost 1-0, and Haynes was back in the side for the next game, at Burnley, in which Fulham lost 3-0.

LEFT: Alan Ball, George Cohen and Ray Wilson, World Cup heroes, before the 1966–67 season opener between Fulham and Everton.

FULHAM FOOTBALL & ATHLETIC CO. LTD.
CRAVEN COTTAGE.

PAGE 18 DAILY MIRROR, Wednesday, December 28, 1966

LEGGAT LASHES HAT-TRICK

Leicester sag as Fulham make it a double

Fulham 4, Leicester 2: by HARRY MILLER

GRAHAM LEGGAT yesterday scored a hat-trick that could see him stride into 1967 as a wanted man. It gave Fulham their fifth win in the last six games.

Graham Leggat, Fulham's hat-trick hero, tumbles backwards after scoring against Leicester, at Craven Cottage.

WALSALL LEADER SENT OFF

Reading 3, Walsall 1

MELIA PLOTS SHOCK UPSET BY SAINTS

Southampton 2, Arsenal 1

Albion knock Spurs out of title chase

By KEN JONES

Spurs 0, WBA 0

IT'S LIGHTS OUT AT LINCOLN

Lincoln 0, Port Vale 1

Bradley boy is a winner for Villa

By PETER INGALL: A Villa 2, Sunderland 1

SWANS LEAVE IT LATE—BUT SNATCH POINT

Shrewsbury 2, Swansea 2

BUMPER GATE—BUT IT'S A BORE

Plymouth 0, Portsmouth 0

Late goal-blitz

Crystal Palace 3, Cardiff 1

TWO GOALS FOR ROWLAND AS MANSFIELD GET REVENGE

Mansfield 3, Scunthorpe 1

SHEFFIELD GRABS A POINT

Norwich 1, Millwall 1

Notts Co 2, Rochdale 0

Newport 3, Exeter 2

On 5th November Fulham lost 6-1 at West Ham but then won seven of the next nine games, a run that undoubtedly kept them in the division. After the first of these, a 5-1 win over Villa, Vic Buckingham gave an insight into some of his man-management techniques: "You know I was getting the bird from the crowd in the first half, and during the interval I told Mark [Pearson] that it was because I put him in the team. He did well after that."

Two weeks later Fulham beat Manchester City 4-1. George Cohen put the Whites ahead from 35 yards, but City equalized, and Cohen had to deliver some home truths to his colleagues: "I started to yell at the younger members of the forward line – Steve Earle, Les Barrett and Allan Clarke – to run more off the ball. Once they got the message the goals started coming."

Clarke, in particular, was in the middle of a purple patch: the young striker scored twice in four of the last five home games.

Fulham emerged from the relegation zone after a 3-1 win over Southampton (Clarke two, Conway one) on 10th December, then beat Leicester City twice in two days after Christmas, Graham Leggat scoring a hat-trick in the second game, a 4-2 win.

LEFT: Home to Spurs. After this, the 10th game of the season, Fulham were in the relegation places with five points from 10 games. They lost 4-3, and Tony Macedo went to hospital with a fractured jaw and a broken tooth.

ABOVE: Fulham players on the swings after training was abandoned in London before the team's FA Cup Fourth Round replay against Sheffield United. When the game did go ahead Fulham lost 3-1.

LEFT: Robson and Ian St John during a 2-2 draw at the Cottage in late February.

1967–68 *Things Fall Apart*

If 1958–59 had been the season when Fulham's greatest side started to put it all together, 1967–68 was the season when Fulham fell apart. Haynes had his 33rd birthday in October, Robson, Leggat and Mullery had been sold, and George Cohen's career would soon be ended by injury. Few teams could survive the loss of such talent, and so relegation came and the golden days were over.

There were good results along the way, but 1967–68 also saw three separate winless streaks of at least six games, and the Whites ended up conceding 98 goals, which tells its own story.

Vic Buckingham's contract was not renewed and Bobby Robson came back from Canada to take over.

The lone positive was young Allan Clarke, who scored 27 goals in all competitions. If Fulham were to have any chance of rebounding they needed to build around young players of Clarke's stature; but instead he was sold to Leicester City for £150,000.

RIGHT: Vic Buckingham watches Steve Earle run laps.

ABOVE: A bobble-hatted Buckingham, poised to start or stop something.

Fulham, who finished bottom, against Manchester City, who finished top.

In manager Robson's opinion Fulham were City's equals for an hour, but then conceded a penalty and lost it from there. "We folded up and made it easy for City," he said. "Had we kept on playing as we had been we might have pegged the score at 3-1 or even pulled a goal or two back. Instead we left the impression that we were overwhelmed. We weren't." Fulham lost 5-1!

RED ROSE

Charlie Rum
THRELFALLS PARKSIDE HOTEL
VOLKSWAGEN

LOOKERS for AUSTINS

In April, Fulham lost to Manchester United twice in four days: 4-0 at home and 3-0 away. Here, Denis Law scores at the Cottage.

Law scores for United at Old Trafford.

PAGE 26 DAILY MIRROR, Saturday, April 13, 1968

SOUTHWELL N H

THURSDAY'S WINNERS

YESTERDAY'S SPORTS SUMMARY

CARLISLE HINTS

Four-goal United go back on top—and Law joins in the rout of the disbelievers

THE FANS SING: GOODBYE, FULHAM

MANCHESTER UNITED are again in front of the cluster of clubs battling towards the championship.

Fulham 0 Man U 4 By HARRY MILLER

Congratulations for Denis Law after scoring United's fourth

Unwelcome visitors at Anfield?

'WE'RE RUNNING OUT OF PLAYERS'—QPR

QPR 1, Cardiff 0: By NIGEL CLARKE

Charlton pull away from the bottom

Dropped

ENGLAND YOUTH OUT

HAMMERS FIND IT ALL SO SIMPLE

West Ham 3, Nottm. Forest 0

HESLOP DEFIES CHELSEA, THEN BEATS THEM!

The Perishers

After the Glory
1968-1997

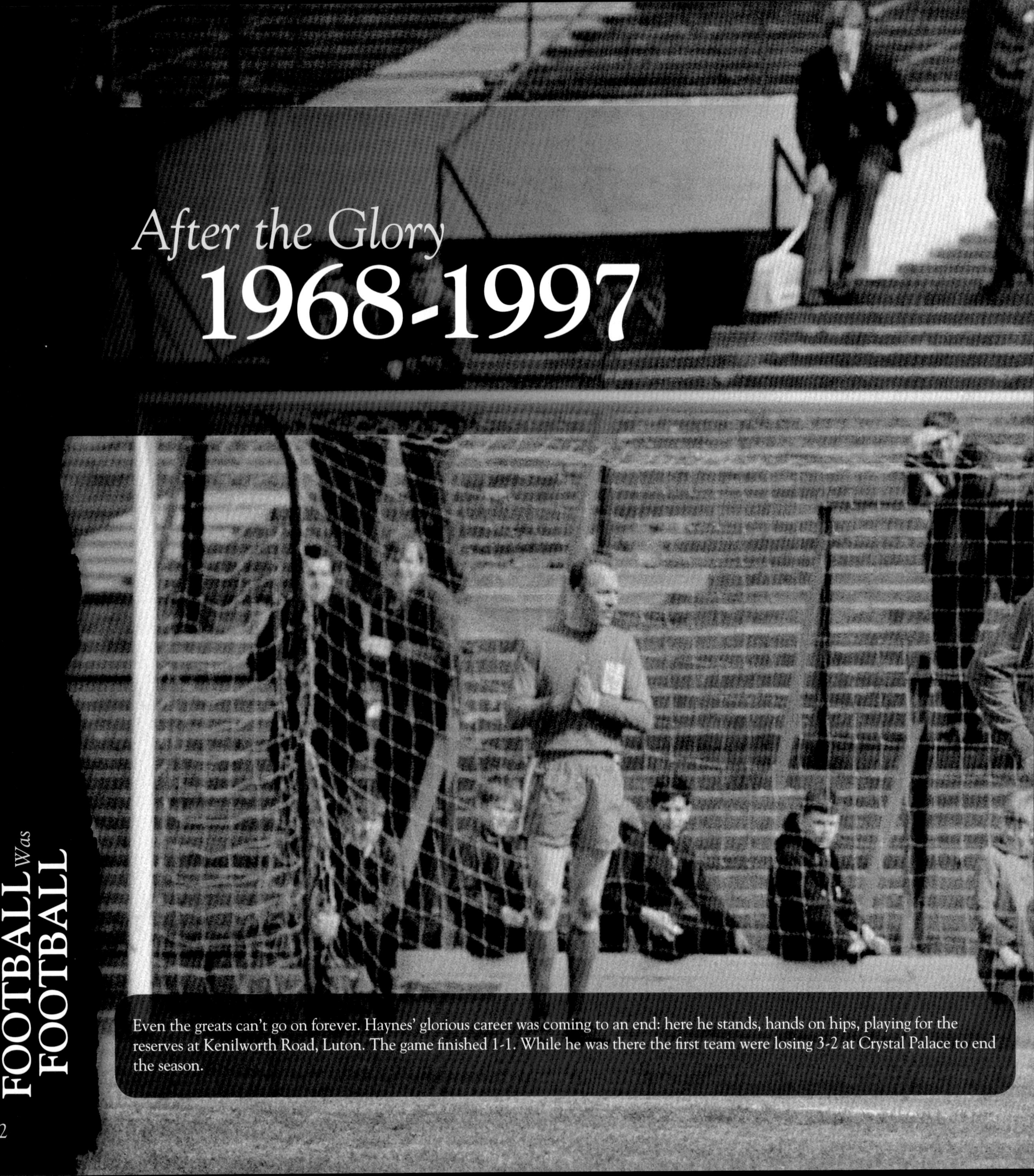

Even the greats can't go on forever. Haynes' glorious career was coming to an end: here he stands, hands on hips, playing for the reserves at Kenilworth Road, Luton. The game finished 1-1. While he was there the first team were losing 3-2 at Crystal Palace to end the season.

The post-war period really had been a golden era for Fulham. It couldn't last forever, and relegation from the First Division in 1968 hit the club hard. Fulham in the Seventies were more entertaining than successful; Fulham in the 1980s almost ceased to exist.

April 1969, Craven Cottage: Johnny Haynes' benefit match.

In 1968–69 Fulham went down again. There was a feeling of disarray about Fulham. Bobby Robson's management didn't seem to be working out, in part, says Malcolm Macdonald (who had just broken into the first team), because the club's senior players were undermining their manager.

Robson, Macdonald suggests, had decided that many of his current side were past their best (including Haynes, whom Robson had dropped at times), and wanted to give youth its chance. In a training session shortly before he was sacked, Robson set up what appeared to be a 'young' v 'old' practice match, and it was thought that the younger side would form the majority of the starting XI in the next game.

It didn't happen, because Robson was sacked before it could. Robson read about rumours of his dismissal on newspaper hoardings on Putney High Street, then arrived at the ground the next day to find that he was indeed out of a job. This was November 1968: Robson had only taken over in January that year, so his pleas for more time were reasonable. Against that, the team were bottom of the league again and facing a second straight relegation.

Haynes took over temporarily, then handed the job on to Bill Dodgin Jr. At the start of March Dodgin dropped Haynes for the remainder of the season, suggesting that Robson hadn't been wrong in his assessment of the side.

One fallout from the Robson dismissal was the departure of Macdonald. The young forward, who went on to become an England international, was sold to Luton Town before he'd really had a chance in the Fulham team. Macdonald had been a Robson signing and after the change of management hadn't had much of a look in the first team, despite making a promising start. Macdonald was desperate for a pay rise (he was on less than he had been as a non-league player) and had to move to get it. It wasn't long since the club had let Allan Clarke move on, and while neither player wanted to stay (for different reasons), it's still hard not to wonder what might have been achieved had they remained Fulham players.

January 1968: Bobby Robson back, in charge, but uneasy.

Pelé and his wife Rosa, bewildered in England.

When Pelé came to Craven Cottage

Fulham 2-Santos 1

Strange as it may seem, Fulham hosted Brazilian club Santos for a friendly in March 1973. The star attraction was Pelé, no longer a Brazil player but still in his early thirties. Pelé did not overexert himself in the game, but still managed a goal, converting a penalty after he himself had been fouled. Alan Pinkney and Steve Earle scored for Fulham.

Santos were a novelty, but not especially good guests. Fulham's Secretary, Graham Hortop, was not impressed. "Their visit brought us all manner of difficulties. We gave them a copy of our gate returns but they insisted there were more people in the ground than we said. It's monstrous that a foreign club can be allowed to get away with this sort of thing."

Plymouth Argyle, Santos' other opponents on this trip, supported Hortop's concerns. Chairman Bob Daniel said "Santos behaved disgracefully. We had to pay them another £2,000, otherwise the match would have been called off with 38,000 people already in the ground. Half an hour before the start Santos were prepared to walk out and I had to accept their blackmail and pay them."

Coke
Coke

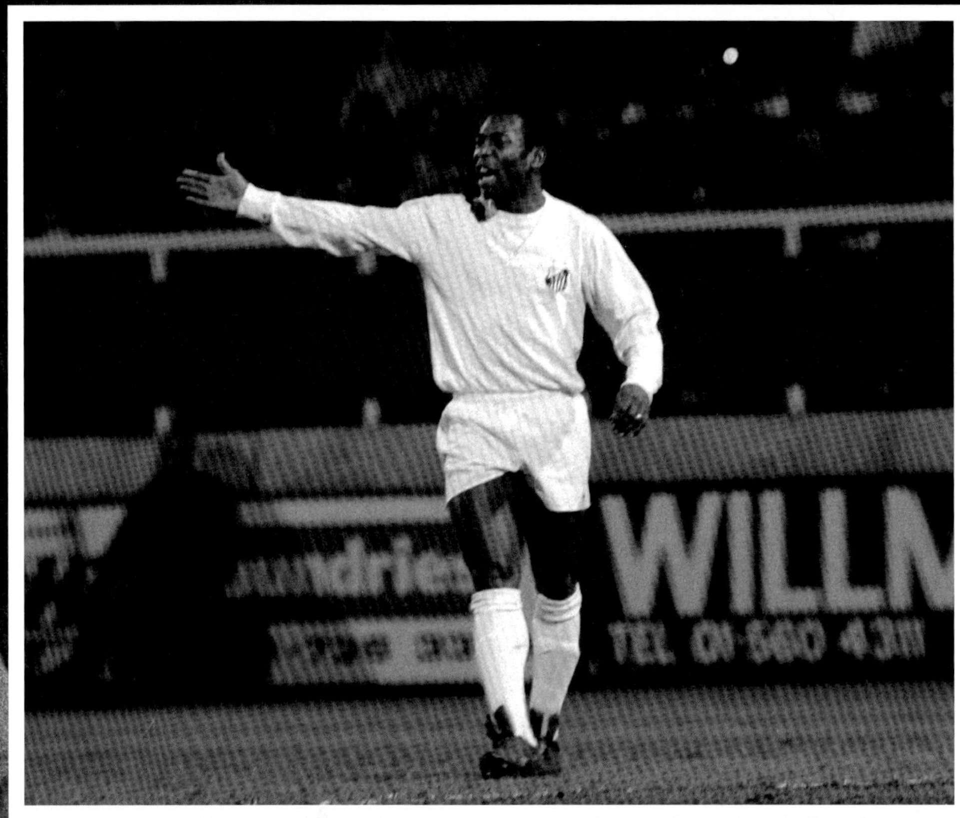
WILLM

20th January 1974: 15,143 people turned up to watch Millwall beat Fulham 1-0. Nothing unusual in that, except that this was the first ever English league match to be played on a Sunday.

In 1974 Fulham signed former England captain Bobby Moore. Moore was unsettled at West Ham and Alan Mullery was asked to sound him out about joining Fulham. Mullery's pitch was successful, and Moore went on to play 150 times for the Whites. Highlights included the famous 1975 FA Cup run, in which he was hugely influential.

ABOVE: Fulham v WBA 1974: Moore climbs high.

1975: *The FA Cup run*

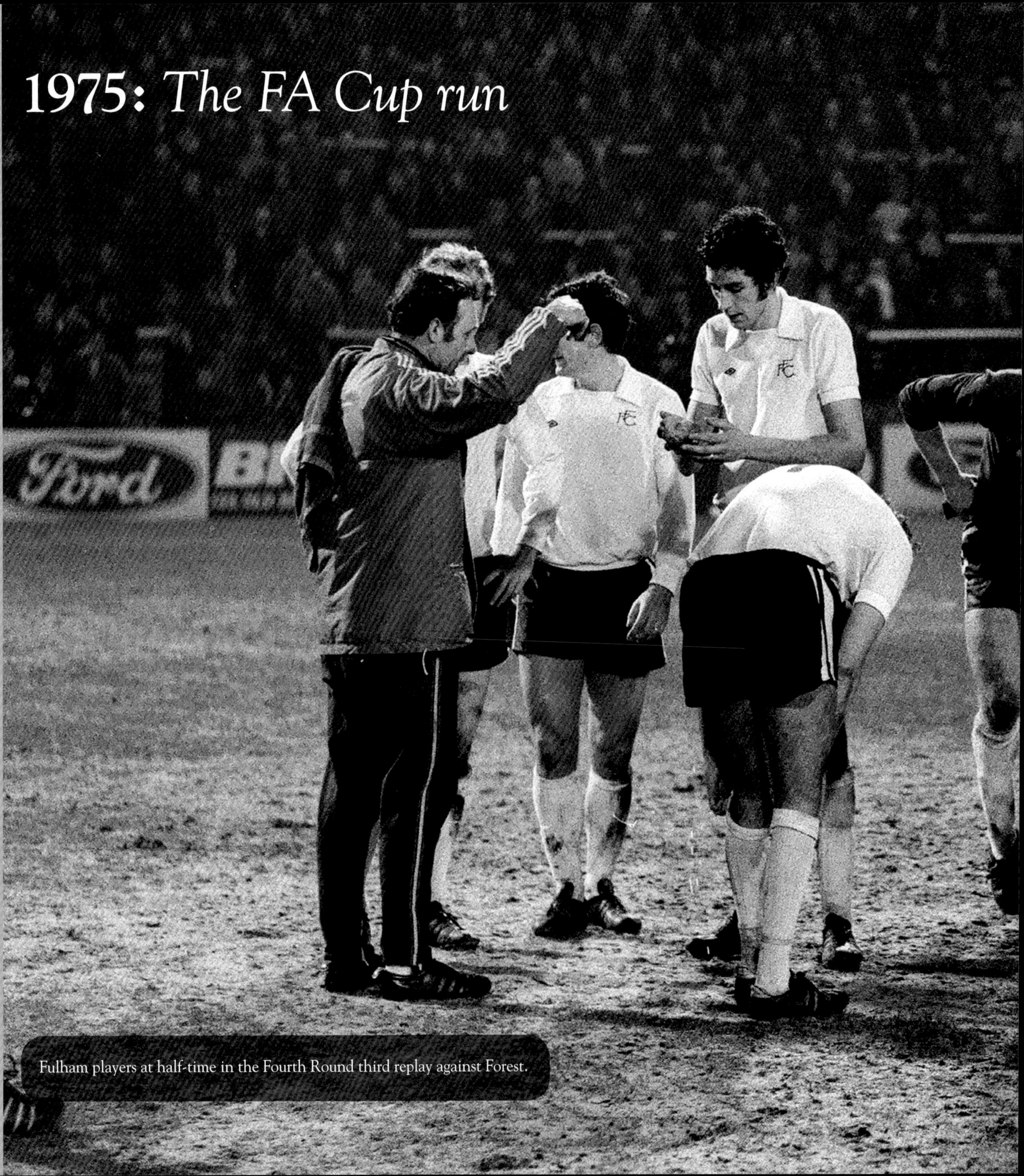

Fulham players at half-time in the Fourth Round third replay against Forest.

Fulham's Cup run started gently enough with a 1-1 home draw with Hull City. Alan Mullery expressed annoyance that the Whites hadn't won a game they'd dominated: "we did enough in the first 30 minutes to wrap it up". Jimmy Conway scored for Fulham, Ken Wagstaff equalized for Hull.

Fulham nearly blew it in the replay, too. After again dominating the early exchanges, Fulham could have scored four in the first 25 minutes. As it was, Viv Busby finally broke the deadlock on 64 minutes, but Hull's Peter Fletcher intercepted a Les Strong backpass soon after, and made it 1-1. A Stuart Croft goal put Hull 2-1 up in extra time, but Busby nabbed a last-minute equalizer to force a second replay.

This game was staged at a neutral ground, Filbert Street in Leicester. Fewer than 5,000 fans (from both sides combined) made the journey, but one man who did see the game was Brian Clough, whose Nottingham Forest side was to play the winner of this game in the Fourth Round. The game was settled by a single goal, Busby's cross missed by everybody before striking the Hull right-back on the knee and bouncing into the net.

FA Cup Third Round second replay v Hull City, at Filbert Street, Leicester.

DAILY MIRROR, Tuesday, February 11, 1975 PAGE 27

FA CUP SPECIAL

FULHAM, AT LAST!

Busby's two goals end the marathon

VIV BUSBY brought football's longest-running saga to an end by firing the goals that carried Fulham safely through last night's F A Cup fourth round third replay.

Busby swooped to score once in each half to shatter Brian Clough's Forest and take Fulham to Everton in the next round. Both the goals were set up by Fulham skipper Alan Mullery, who had a magnificent match in midfield.

By JACK STEGGLES
Nott'm Forest 1, Fulham 2

The first came in the twenty-sixth minute. Mullery split the Forest defence with a short, sharp pass. Jim Conway turned the ball back across the face of the goal, and Busby did the rest.

Then nine minutes into the second-half, Mullery left Forest floundering with a gloriously-struck forty-yard through ball. Blistering pace carried Busby away from Paul Richardson, and he dribbled round goalkeeper John Middleton before firing home.

Superior

Fulham showed such a clear superiority that most neutral observers were left wondering why they needed four matches before winning. They were forced to soak up a lot of pressure from a Forest side which lacked nothing when it came to effort. But Forest were woefully short of ideas, and the Fulham defence — superbly held together by the masterly Bobby Moore—had little trouble in turning back the wave of attacks.

Moore, still looking every inch an England player, turned in the sort of commanding display that had Clough—one of his greatest admirers—drooling with envy.

Fulham had few anxious moments. First, Ian Bowyer escaped early on to blaze a short-range effort against the bar. Then John Lacy hooked the ball off the line after Bowyer had beaten Peter Mellor.

From the corner Bob Chapman raised Forest hopes briefly by jabbing in their sixty-first minute consolation goal. But in contrast to Forest's frenzied efforts, Fulham looked dangerous whenever they counter-attacked.

Mullery told me: "Justice has been done at last. We have played Forest six times in the last couple of months, and have murdered them on five occasions without getting the ball in the net.

"We have a very young side who are quite excited at the prospect of playing the First Division leaders. But it's also a marvellous feeling for old 'uns like Bobby Moore and myself."

Short

Forest boss Clough agreed that Fulham were the better side.

"We are a bit short of skill, aren't we?" he said. "Despite all the pressure we applied, we did not create a thing.

"In a way, I'm glad we're out of the Cup. Now we can get down to some real work. And there's a lot to be done here."

Viv Busby, Fulham's hero, beats Forest goalkeeper John Middleton for his second goal in last night's F A Cup replay at Nottingham and earn Fulham a fifth round trip to First Division Everton on Saturday. Picture: DICK WILLIAMS

SPEEDWAY

Anders breaks leg in holiday trial ride

By GRAHAM BAKER

WORLD champion Anders Michanek, never seriously injured in ten years of speedway racing, has broken his left leg on holiday in Australia.

Swedish star Michanek also needed twenty stitches in the leg after falling from a trial bike.

He is expected to stay in hospital for several days and will be out of speedway for months.

Reading, who were hoping to sign Michanek, could now try for Wolverhampton's Ole Olsen.

SPURS CRISIS

UNHAPPY PETERS MAY SEEK MOVE

MARTIN PETERS will talk over his future with Tottenham manager Terry Neill, in a showdown meeting tomorrow.

By NIGEL CLARKE

And it could lead to a transfer request from the unsettled Spurs captain, who was upset at being substituted in the 2-0 home defeat by Stoke on Saturday.

Norwich manager John Bond will be watching the situation closely. He has been an admirer of Peters for some time and would be interested in signing him.

Peters had planned to see Neill yesterday, but the Spurs boss went to Scotland to check on Rangers striker Derek Parlane and Aberdeen centre half Willie Young in the Cup replay at Ibrox Park.

Neill, who recently signed John Duncan from Dundee, is ready to buy in Scotland again to halt Spurs' slump.

D-Day for sent-off Cruyff

THE Spanish Football Federation is expected to decide today what punishment to hand out to Dutch super-star Johan Cruyff, Soccer's latest bad boy.

Armed police had to be called on to the pitch to escort off Cruyff after being sent off.

Backed up by fellow Barcelona players, the £1 million Dutchman at first refused to go after being shown the red card during Sunday's 3—2 defeat at Malaga.

He was protesting about Malaga's second goal.

SWINDON STAR IS BANNED

Millwall escape punishment for knife-thrower

MILLWALL escaped punishment when they answered charges of crowd misbehaviour before an FA disciplinary commission in London yesterday.

The hearing followed an incident at The Den on December 7 when a knife was thrown on to the pitch and struck an Orient player.

After hearing from Millwall chairman Herbert Bunridge and two police officers in charge of crowd arrangements, the commission decided to take no further action.

They ruled that all reasonable precautions had been taken and noted that Millwall were planning further measures.

Swindon forward Colin Prophett was cleared when colleague David Moss admitted it was he who made remarks to [illegible] at Plymouth on Boxing Day. Moss's honesty cost him a £50 fine and a three-match suspension.

West Ham left back Frank Lampard escaped a two-match suspension when it was decided not to record a caution against Queen's Park Rangers last month.

Eddie Colquhoun, Sheffield United centre-half, also escaped a two-match ban.

GREYHOUNDS AND SPORTS SUMMARY

FA CUP
Fourth Round Replay
Wimbledon .... 0 Leeds Utd. 1
Bassett (o g)
45,701
H-T: 0—0
(at Selhurst Park; Leeds away to Derby in Fifth Round)

Fourth Round, Third Replay

TONIGHT'S SOCCER

DAILY MIRROR LEISURE GUIDE

CINEMAS

The Fourth Round tie was difficult. Forest played what Clough described as "more good football in this match than in any other game since I took over," and Bill Taylor, Fulham's coach, agreed. "That's the worst we have played this season, and it's no good blaming the pitch," he said (the pitch had required eight hours work to make it playable). "Our front men never got a kick, and someone's in for a right rollicking."

Les Barrett hit the bar after a 60-yard run, and Viv Busby headed just over, but that was that as far as Fulham chances went.

The replay at Forest also finished 1-1 (John Dowie scored), so the teams were back at the Cottage for another 120 minutes of hard football. Brian Clough suggested that "if nobody wins on Monday we ought to line both teams up against a wall and shoot them."

Again Fulham were the better side, and hit the woodwork twice. Les Barrett came particularly close to settling the tie with only five minutes of extra time left, but John Middleton in the Forest goal somehow kept out his point-blank header.

Fulham scored early when Jimmy Conway crossed and the ball found its way to Alan Slough, who shot home from 18 yards. Forest equalized with a John Robertson free-kick, but soon Fulham were on top again. Barrett broke clean through, but shot wide, then the same player hit the bar. Extra time saw more of the same, but Fulham couldn't score. "This tie has become a slogging match now and we are dealing with very tired players," said Alec Stock. "We have played each other so many times now we are like friends, not enemies."

The marathon finally ended after a third replay. A nice move involving Moore and Conway left Busby with a simple chance to make it 1-0. Then in the second half a 40-yard Mullery through ball put Busby clear again, and he rounded Middleton and scored his second. Forest scored a consolation after 61 minutes, but after that Fulham were able to soak up the Forest pressure and frequently threatened on the break.

"Justice has been done at last," said Alan Mullery. "We have played Forest six times in the last couple of months, and have murdered them on five occasions without getting the ball in the net. We have a very young side who are quite excited about the prospect of playing the First Division leaders [Everton, who lay in wait]. But it's also a marvellous feeling for old 'uns like Bobby Moore and myself." Both players had outstanding games. Brian Clough agreed: "We are a bit short of skill, aren't we? Despite all the pressure we applied, we did not create a thing."

FA Cup Fourth Round v Forest, at home. The tie went to three replays before Fulham won the match.

Peter Mellor in flight during the first Forest game.

FA Cup Fourth Round replay away to Forest.

Moore and Mellor deal with the danger: FA Cup Fourth Round, third replay.

Viv Busby celebrates. He scored twice as the Whites finally got past Forest.

April 1975, Fulham v Chelsea charity match in aid of Police Dependents Trust Fund.

Busby was at it again in the next round at high flying Everton, scoring twice to put Fulham through to the quarter-finals. "We've beaten Everton who were top of the First Division, and we're in the last eight, so we have a real chance of getting to the final," he said afterwards. He wasn't so excited about the draw for the next round though, Carlisle away. "It wouldn't have been so bad if we'd had them at home. Not that we're not confident. When you've won at Everton, why be afraid of going to Carlisle?" His first came when Dai Davies, the Everton goalkeeper, collided with one of his defenders after 16 minutes, and while Roger Kenyon equalized early in the second half, Busby scored again late on with a shot on the turn.

The win over Carlisle was (at the time) manager Alec Stock's proudest moment in football. "I've been through a hell of a lot in football, but nothing has given me more satisfaction. In 58 years I never thought this would ever happen to me. I'm walking on air. I came to the club to put it back on its feet. When the final whistle went I thought at last we are on our way to achieving something."

It was a tough game. Fulham scored in the 67th minute through Les Barrett, their only shot of the game, but Carlisle piled on the pressure for the rest of the match. Peter Mellor had to be at his best in the Fulham goal and Moore and Mullery, as they had been throughout the Cup run, were immense.

When Jimmy Conway went down with a head injury, Stock went to see how he was. Moore strolled across, asking Stock how he was doing. "When I told him not very well he said 'Relax, it's well under control. There's no need to worry.' What a man!"

Moore was thrilled after the final whistle. "It was a magical moment. I never dreamed this would happen to me again. I thought events like this belonged in my past."

Mullery was relieved. "I'll be the first to admit that waiting for the final whistle was terrible. I never thought it would come."

In the semi-final Fulham drew 1-1 with Birmingham, John Mitchell's wonder strike being quickly cancelled out by a scruffy Joe Gallagher goal. Coach Billy Taylor described this as follows: "The ball scraped off Bobby Moore's head, went through John Lacy's legs, Alan Slough just missed it, and Gallagher got on the end of that little lot." Birmingham's manager Freddie Goodwin complained that this was the worst his side had played all season, which annoyed Alan Mullery. "It's funny. You play First Division sides, they don't do so well against you, and they say they had an off day. They don't say Fulham played ever so well. If we get to Wembley we won't disgrace the place."

In the build-up to the replay, Mullery was even more bullish. "I can't see us losing. We'll get to Wembley. I get the needle when I read that Birmingham can't play as badly again. Why can't they? To be honest I can't see anyone in the City side who can lift them to a better performance."

Another 120-minute marathon followed. With 10 seconds left in extra time John Mitchell stretched to turn a flick on goalwards, then, when that was saved, somehow found it in himself to get to the rebound first and divert it home. In the dressing room Mullery climbed on a table and raised a toast. Signalling towards Moore, Mullery simply said "Thank you for taking two old men back to Wembley again."

Two old men: Moore and Mullery get into the Cup final spirit with some publicity photos.

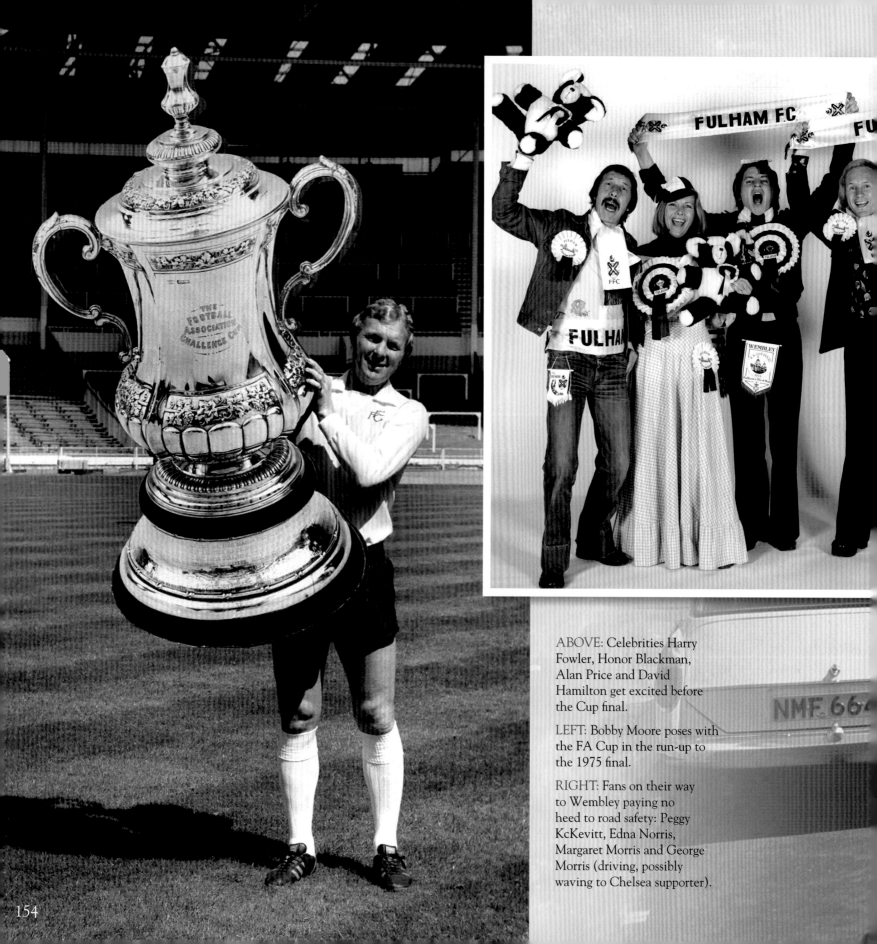

ABOVE: Celebrities Harry Fowler, Honor Blackman, Alan Price and David Hamilton get excited before the Cup final.

LEFT: Bobby Moore poses with the FA Cup in the run-up to the 1975 final.

RIGHT: Fans on their way to Wembley paying no heed to road safety: Peggy KcKevitt, Edna Norris, Margaret Morris and George Morris (driving, possibly waving to Chelsea supporter).

-LEGENDS-

Alan Mullery

Alan Mullery broke into the Fulham side as a teenager and played through the club's glory seasons until he was sold to Spurs behind manager Bedford Jezzard's back in 1964.

In retrospect that was the beginning of the end for Fulham: Jezzard walked out as a result of this, Vic Buckingham's tenure didn't really work out, and Fulham flirted with relegation for some time before finally succumbing in 1968.

Mullery played an important part in England's 1970 World Cup side (arguably as good as the 1966 side) and won the FA Cup, the League Cup and the UEFA Cup with Spurs.

Strangely, he found himself out of favour at Spurs soon after raising the UEFA Cup, and was told to find himself a new club. Crystal Palace offered him the best deal, but Fulham manager Alec Stock convinced him to return to Fulham by offering a sort of managerial apprenticeship, the idea being that Mullery would take over from Stock after four years. But when the four years were up Stock changed his mind and Mullery was left high and dry.

Amid all this Mullery won the Football Writers Association Footballer of the Year award for 1974–75, and was instrumental in bringing Bobby Moore to Fulham. The pair of them were, of course, vital to the club's 1975 FA Cup run.

FOOTBALL -STATS-

Alan Mullery

Name: Alan Mullery

Born: London 1941

Position: Midfield

Fulham playing career: 1958–1976 (elsewhere 1965–1970)

Appearances: 412

Goals: 42

England appearances: 35

Goals: 1

In the build-up to the FA Cup final Alan Mullery was voted Footballer of the Year. He said "I thought getting to the final was tremendous, but this takes my breath away." Alec Stock added "Quite the nicest thing to happen to Fulham this season. Alan deserves it, he's a tremendous captain."

On the eve of the final Fulham's preparations were thrown out of the window by a surprise visitor. A representative of Stylo Matchmakers, a Leeds-based boot company, burst into the players' dining room issuing writs to everyone present. The players then learned that Alec Stock had signed a contract at the start of the season, and that if the players didn't agree to wear Stylo boots the Cup final would be cancelled because of a court order restraining the players from wearing boots (or carrying hold-alls) made by companies other than Stylo.

Coach Bill Taylor said that "Stylo have spoken to me, and all the players, except Bobby Moore, will wear their boots. Moore did not sign any contract."

After a bad night's sleep, the players reconvened in the morning and sent Les Strong, who was injured, to a 10.30 a.m. court hearing. He reported that the final was on, but that the Fulham players had to wear the boots as contracted.

Understandably, the players weren't about to do that, so instead had to paint over the stripes on their preferred boots to keep everyone happy – not the best preparation for the biggest game some of the team would ever play.

CUP FINAL SOCCERSCOPE ON FULHAM

VIV BUSBY
Another attacker who scorns the obvious. Likes to run at defences. Good ball control, quick.

JOHN MITCHELL
Full of confidence following semi-final. Eagerness to take defenders on could unsettle West Ham.

JIMMY CONWAY
Neat, thoughtful forward who makes intelligent breaks from the right. Could be the key figure if fully fit.

JOHN LACY
Uses his height to maximum advantage. Intelligent central defender who has clearly benefited from playing with Bobby Moore.

JOHN CUTBUSH
Aggressive full back who likes to attack down the right flank. Competitive and sensible.

PETER MELLOR
Big and agile, his confidence has grown out of a brilliant Cup run. Has made critical saves in every round. His concentration has improved.

LES BARRETT
Uses devastating pace to turn defences. Centres well with both feet. Could be the match-winner if he concentrates.

ALAN MULLERY
Driving force in the centre of the field. Inspirational leader who can score exceptional goals from long range.

ALAN SLOUGH
Disciplined marker. Great stamina. Could be used to counter Trevor Brooking.

JOHN FRASER
Right-footed full back who might prefer the other flank. Strong, he supports well.

BOBBY MOORE
Once the world's best defender and still shows evidence of it. Outstanding technique, marvellously cool. Responds to the big occasion.

AN EXCLUSIVE CUT OUT AND FILE GUIDE

The teams walk across the famous Wembley track.

In the event Fulham didn't turn up. Peter Mellor had been outstanding on the way to the final, especially at Carlisle when he won the game almost single-handed, but he made two mistakes at Wembley and Fulham lost 2-0. Twice he made handling errors from difficult, hard-hit shots, twice Alan Taylor pounced to score. If these spills weren't quite as bad as has since been made out, he still should have done better. As should his team-mates. Fulham had given everything to get to the final; to lose so quietly was a numbing anti-climax.

The introductions.

RIGHT: Les Barrett. Note the blacked out boots.

RIGHT: Mullery on the ball.

BELOW: Moore in command.

BELOW. Commiserations.

Derby days **1976**

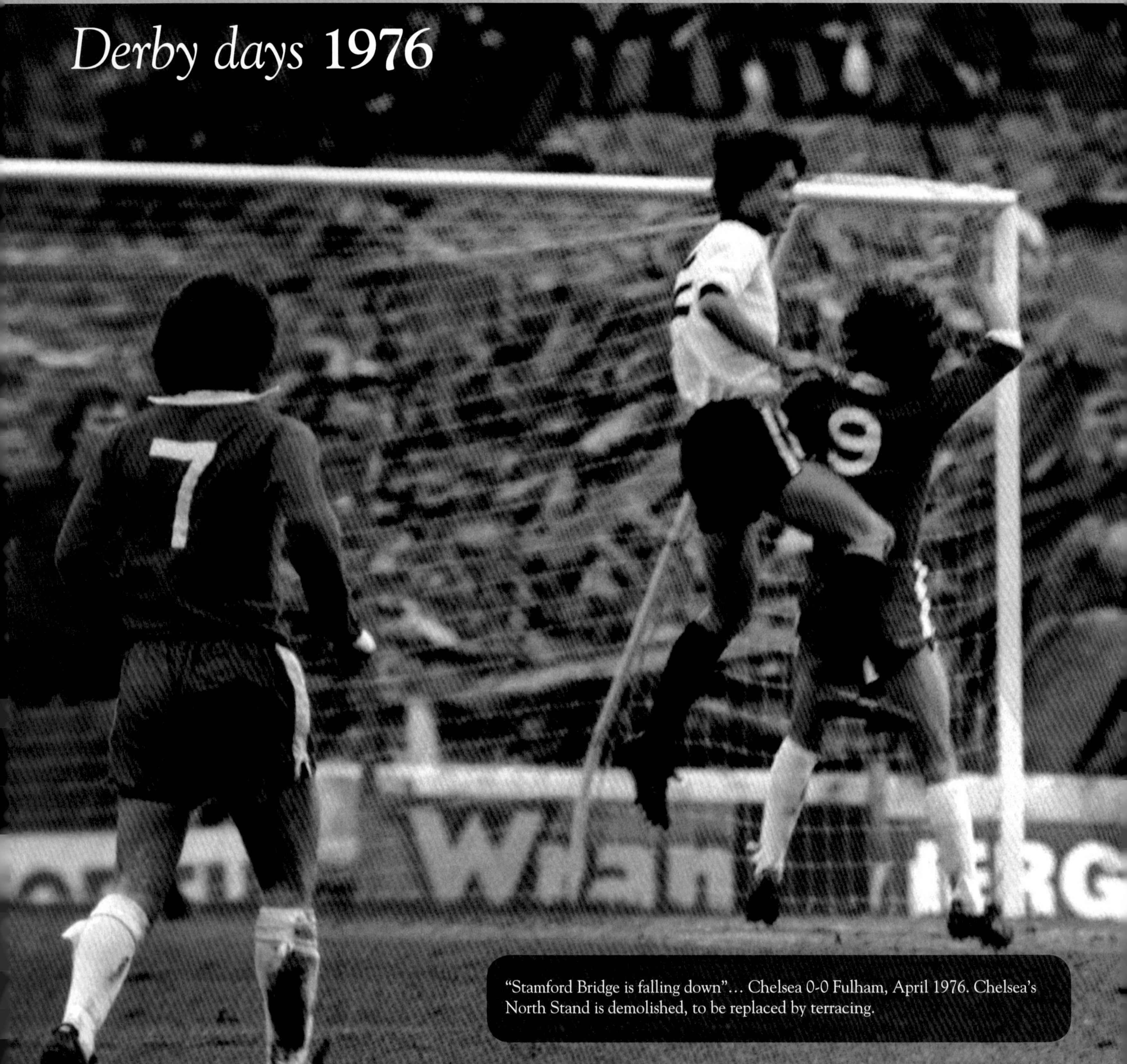

“Stamford Bridge is falling down”… Chelsea 0-0 Fulham, April 1976. Chelsea’s North Stand is demolished, to be replaced by terracing.

R
ICY

October 1976: controversy in the League Cup, as Bobby Moore was sent off in a Third Round replay at Bolton. The game was 97 minutes old when Bolton equalized, and nobody could remember any major stoppages in the second half that justified the injury time. Moore approached the referee at the start of the first period of extra time and, after a short discussion, was shown a red card.

He was followed off the pitch by his team-mates. The referee, Kevin McNally, warned Fulham that they had two minutes to get back onto the field or the game was void. Coach Bobby Campbell led the team back out.

Manager Alec Stock said later, "When a man can't tell the time it's time we all packed in."

Next day Moore clarified his side of the discussion. "I asked why he had played so much time over and if anybody had been injured. He replied that nobody had been hurt… then he sent me off. I was flabbergasted. You have to appreciate our situation. We had battled very hard to keep in the lead and when Bolton equalized during the time the referee added on it was a very bitter pill to swallow."

Kevin McNally was not well supported by his own mother, who said "He's always been mad on all kinds of sport but he has never played any of them." Mrs McNally continued: "Kevin is always firm, even with me. If I do anything wrong in the shop he tells me off. He is a man who sticks by his decision."

Fulham lost the second replay at St Andrew's, Birmingham, 2-1.

George Best

George Best had been playing in the ageing-star-laden NASL in the USA when the chance arose to return to England with Fulham. He'd enjoyed his time in Los Angeles, where expectation and pressure were low. His health, which had suffered in his later Manchester United years, was improving. He was happy. The chance to play in a good part of London, on decent wages, with a flat and car thrown in, was very appealing.

Before his debut against Bristol Rovers, Best noted that he was "as excited as when I played my first match for Manchester United. I can't wait to get started."

He didn't hang around, scoring within 90 seconds of his debut with a swerving 20-yard drive that Rovers goalkeeper Jim Eadie misjudged. After that he faded, but a crowd of 21,500 – double Fulham's usual gate – went home satisfied. Rovers defender Frank Prince, who had marked Best, was a little disappointed though. "Best wasn't as good as I thought he'd be. I expected he'd be sharper and fitter."

Best did indeed need a bit of time to get up to speed, but the quality was there for all to see. Against Peterborough in a midweek League Cup tie he scored again, this time a delicious volley from 25 yards after he'd flicked the ball into the air himself. "I got a real kick from seeing that one go in. It's the most satisfying goal I've scored for a long time," said Best.

Fulham were delighted, too. Against Wolves in the next game 25,794 came to watch, a huge crowd for the Second Division at the time.

Balance: Best on the run against Burnley.

But it didn't last. Best was sent off against Southampton for using foul language. Fulham argued that in this case a number of players should have gone, but the referee, a policeman from Torquay, was unmoved. "I did my job," he said. Fulham went six games without a win after that, and behind the scenes Best was starting to go back to his old ways. He felt that Fulham had been slow in paying his signing-on fee, and wasn't impressed with his club flat. He started drinking heavily again.

Fulham were in a difficult position, and Best was delighted with the way manager Campbell accepted his lifestyle. "It was no good trying to keep me at home. If Manchester United couldn't do it, Fulham weren't going to, were they?" Despite all this he still performed well enough to win the Supporters' Player of the Year award.

After he returned to America for the summer Best decided that he didn't want to come back to England after all. In the event Fulham got 10 more games out of him, but soon he was back on a plane to Los Angeles, and that was that.

Training.

Tumbling.

Gliding.

Best and Marsh, Fulham's entertainers.

Rodney Marsh emerged at Fulham as a young player, making his debut as a teenager. But he didn't work well with Haynes, a problem for any Fulham player, and manager Vic Buckingham didn't feel things were working out. So Marsh was sold to QPR. He returned to play with George Best, a combination that certainly appealed to the casual fan and the newsmen, but ultimately this spell was no more successful than his first.

Phenomenally talented, Rodney Marsh never did turn that talent into footballing achievement.

Derby days 1977

April 1977: Chelsea's march towards the First Division shuddered to a halt as they ran into an inspired Fulham team. Chelsea manager Eddie McCreadie confirmed that "It was the worst we have played this season. We have had a long chat about it." Alan Warboys, George Best and John Mitchell scored for the Whites in a 3-1 win.

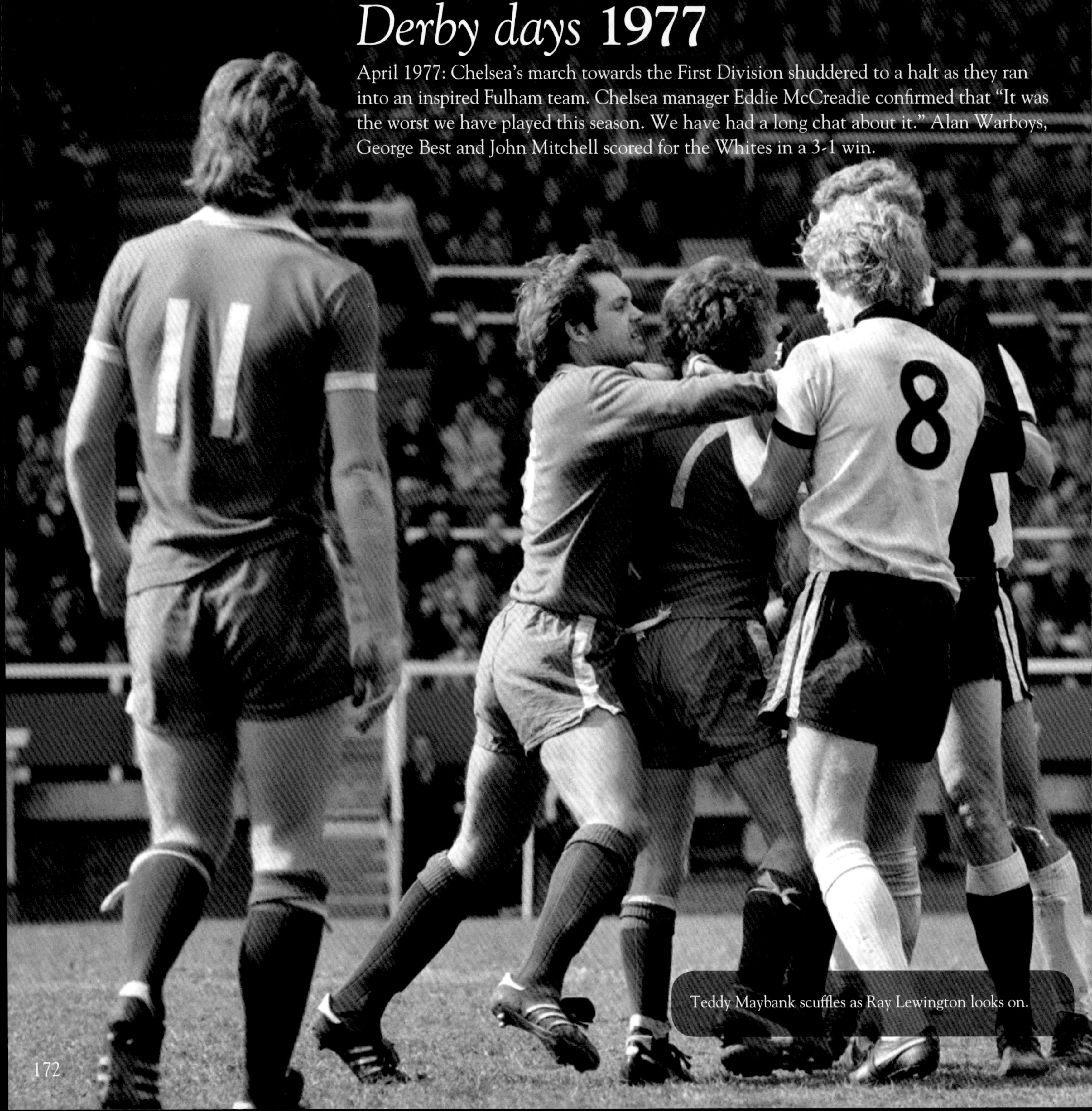

Teddy Maybank scuffles as Ray Lewington looks on.

John Mitchell celebrates his goal.

In 1977 Bobby Moore called it a day. His last game at Craven Cottage was a 6-1 win over Leyton Orient in which Fulham scored six in the first half.

& PARTNERS LTD.
AND PROVINCES

Guard of honour for the great man.

Pre-match attention.

In charge, immaculate.

Derby days 1980

Fulham v Chelsea, March 1980: a 2-1 defeat.

ABOVE: Gerry Peyton comes out bravely.

LEFT: Teddy Maybank again…

Malcolm Macdonald

Malcolm Macdonald initially joined Fulham as Commercial Director in 1979. His responsibility was to raise funds, no easy task at a Second Division club on its way down. When manager Bobby Campbell was sacked in October 1980 Macdonald asked Chairman Ernie Clay if he might be considered as a replacement, explained why this might be a good idea, and got the job.

Macdonald set about freshening the team up, bringing in Roger Thompson as a coach from Arsenal, and drafting young players like Jeff Hopkins and Paul Parker into the first team. He also improved what he already had, notably Tony Gale, who thrived under Macdonald's tutelage.

Fulham gained promotion in that season's last game, at home to Lincoln City. It was a perfect finale: Fulham led Lincoln by a point, so the game's winner would be promoted. A draw would do for Fulham.

Roger Brown, who scored 12 goals that season from centre-back, headed Fulham ahead. Lincoln equalized then piled on the pressure, but in the end Fulham held on. Macdonald's first season as a manager ended in triumph.

Promotion! Fulham 1-Lincoln City 1. It was enough.

SMOKING

The heroic Roger Brown and his manager. Brown scored 12 goals that season from centre-back, a feat he put down to a free-kick routine the team had perfected in training. Tony Gale would take the kick, Dean Coney would make a run, block off Brown's marker, and Brown would score.

Macdonald's second season was almost as successful as his first. In early February Fulham were in third place with 50 points, and Leicester City in fourth on 39. From there the lead dwindled away to nothing. Fulham's form wasn't bad, but they were in fast company by now and there was little margin for error.

Then in late April Leicester won 1-0 at the Cottage – Macdonald says they outran and outfought Fulham – and the lead was down to two points.

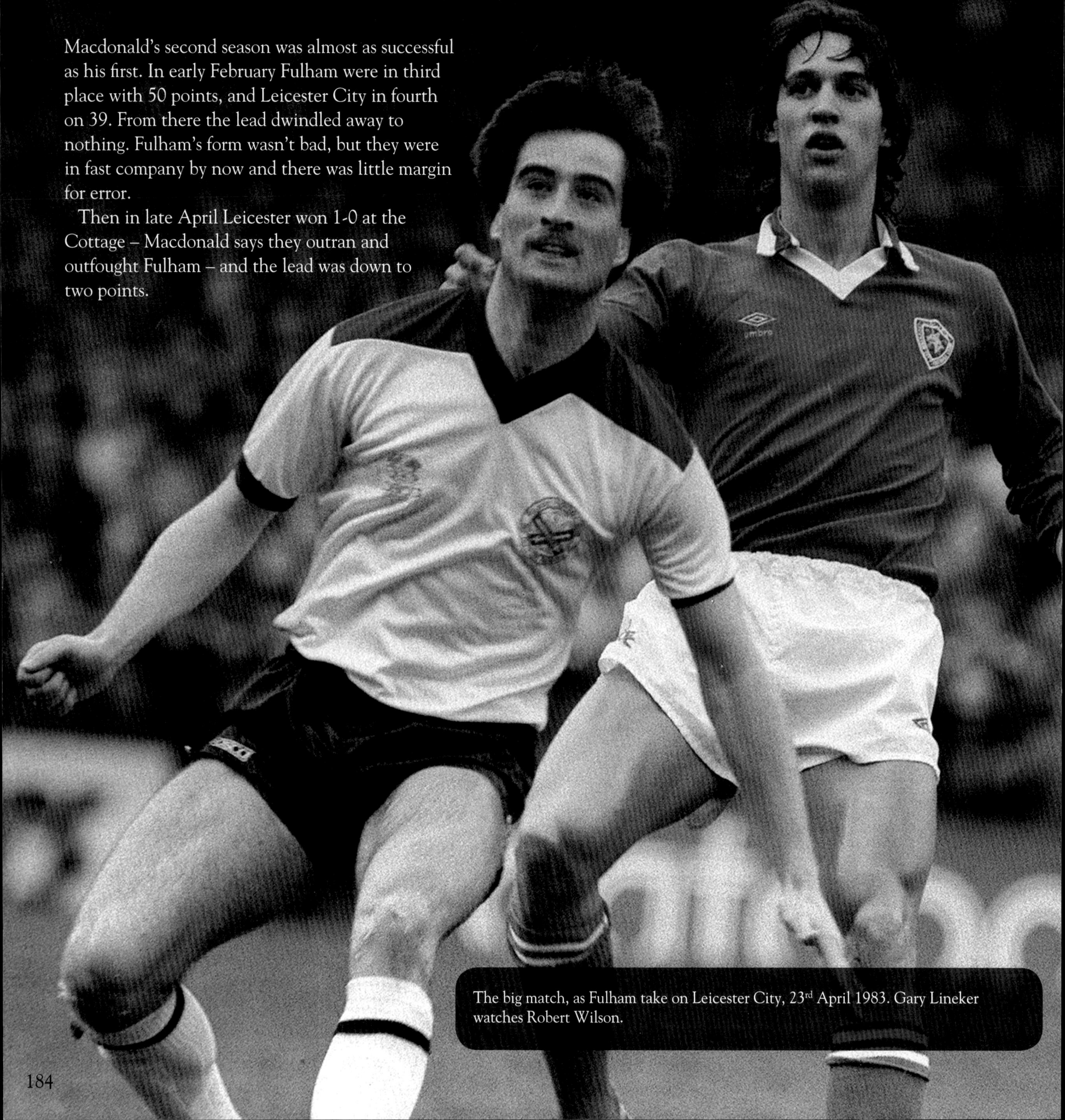

The big match, as Fulham take on Leicester City, 23rd April 1983. Gary Lineker watches Robert Wilson.

It's not happening…

Ray Houghton gives his all.

PAGE 30 DAILY MIRROR, Monday, April 25, 1983

MIRROR SPORT SPECIAL ON THE DRAMA

Mac takes the strain

By HARRY MILLER: Fulham 0, Leicester 1

GORDON MILNE and his Leicester players are taking the softly-softly route to promotion.

It is almost as if they are hoping to arrive in the First Division without anyone noticing.

Talk of promotion, without actually being banned at Filbert Street, is definitely discouraged.

MACDONALD: Testing time ahead. Picture: MONTE FRESCO

Fulham facing real fight now

TOP POSITIONS

Advice

Superb

SPURS FEAR THE WORST

ARDILES

West Bromwich 0, Tottenham 1

THE FEARS Ossie Ardiles has nursed all weekend are likely to be confirmed this morning.

New blow will rule out Ossie

By TERRY SMITH

Ramsey is a risk for Brighton

Brighton 1, Coventry 0

TWO First Division footballers fought each other during a match, which is daft enough.

FLAT OUT: Connor after scoring

FRANK McGHEE

Injured

FIRST DIVISION SOCCER EXTRA —PAGE 29

WALSH KEEN TO GROW UP FAST

By JACK STEGGLES Luton 3, Swansea 1

WALSH: In demand.

Fulham lost at Sheffield Wednesday and QPR, then beat Carlisle, and went into the last game of the season at Derby a point behind Leicester.

Derby needed to win to stay up, so the ground was packed, and a tense game was still 0-0 with 20 minutes to go. Then Derby scored, the crowd ran onto the pitch, and more or less stayed there. Robert Wilson was kicked by a spectator, and Macdonald claimed that six of his players had been roughed up in the chaos. Wilson, Ray Houghton, Jeff Hopkins, Kevin Lock, Roger Brown and John Reeves all made statements to the police.

Fulham's attempts to force an equalizer were thwarted by this extraordinary atmosphere, and to make matters worse the referee blew for full-time at least a minute too soon. Fulham were livid and threatened legal action, but the FA stood firm.

Leicester were promoted, Derby stayed up, and Fulham were left with thoughts of what might have been. Roger Brown blamed the club's failure to sign Brian McDermott from Arsenal on a permanent deal (they wanted £100,000, but Ernie Clay wouldn't pay it), Macdonald blamed the failure to sign Tony Sealy from QPR (Clay wouldn't pay the £75,000 required), but in any case, the team had put in a phenomenal effort and come close to consecutive promotions.

The near miss took its toll, and Fulham sank back into mid-table for the next two seasons. Then it all went horribly wrong.

RIGHT: Malcolm Macdonald helps re-lay the Cottage turf after the season's last home game. Note Ernie Clay's advert on the left-hand side.

Page 30 DAILY MIRROR, Monday, May 16, 1983

END OF THE SOCCER SEASON 83

Troubles pile up for Gould

WHEN Bobby Gould takes over as manager at Coventry today he will be faced by at least eight problems, writes Dave Horridge.

Clough reply is Euro spot

McMahon is Villa target

SPORTS SNAPS

Fulham's Robert Wilson gets a kick on the leg from one of the fans jamming the touchline.

A linesman—squeezed off his line—moves in as Wilson threatens to retaliate in this amazing climax to the season.

JUDGMENT DAY

A FOOTBALL LEAGUE commission will decide today whether Fulham can have another crack at winning promotion from the Second Division.

Fulham set to fight in court

By TONY STENSON

Mirror Sport Comment

HARRY MILLER

SOUR CHAMPERS FOR MILNE MEN

By DAVID MOORE

Deserved

Referee Roy Chadwick catches up with the angry scene—just before deciding to blow the whistle that left the result in doubt.

Pictures by London Weekend Television

DAILY MIRROR, Monday, May 16, 1983 Page 31

Kick that shocked millions

'If F.A. don't vote for replay the mob will take over'

Fulham boss MALCOLM MACDONALD

'I feel quite depressed. It's become a big damp squib'

Leicester boss GORDON MILNE

Ref who can't dodge rumpus

REFEREE Roy Chadwick, the man in the middle of the most explosive end to any soccer season, won't be able to hide from this morning's headlines ... he's a newsagent at Darwen (Lancs), writes Tony Stenson.

UPS AND DOWNS

Lovely finish from Painter stuns Scots

By JACK STEGGLES: England 4, Scotland 2

Rocked

SUMMARY

TOP DOG'S BEST

This year, last year.

–LEGENDS–

Gordon Davies

Gordon "Ivor" Davies' time at Fulham coincided with some of the club's more tricky off-field stretches, but despite this he managed 178 goals in all competitions, a phenomenal record that seems unlikely to be broken.

Davies signed for Manchester City as a schoolboy, but after two seasons he opted to become a teacher, working in Staffordshire. He returned to his home town club, Merthyr Tydfil of the Southern League, and scored 66 goals in 90 games. Fulham beat Cardiff and Swansea to his signature, paying £3,000 up front with a further £2,000 after 20 appearances. After he scored a hat-trick against Birmingham in 1979, Davies told of his relief. "I never thought I would make the grade after failing in a teenage trial with Manchester City and another with Brighton more recently. Fortunately Fulham spotted me in a match for Merthyr Tydfil and gave me my chance. I don't intend to waste it."

He certainly didn't waste his chance, scoring 24 times in the Division Three promotion side. The goals kept on coming, but his ability started to attract the interest of some of the league's top clubs, and Davies understandably wanted an improved contract. This was at a time when Ernie Clay seemed to be tightening his belt and Fulham and Davies could not come to an agreement. Davies was placed on the transfer list and decided to leave the club at the end of his contract.

Chelsea signed him up, but then declined to pay the £300,000 fee Fulham were asking. The deal went to an FA Tribunal, and Clay was livid: "Chelsea haven't had the courtesy to speak to me today. We haven't had any communication since their silly announcement. I feel sorry for Davies. I can see the lad finishing right in the fertiliser. If Chelsea don't take him he will return to us feeling very bitter. He has a better scoring record than Kerry Dixon and Clive Allen and I think we should be paid accordingly and without any hassle."

(It is to be supposed that Clay was not offering to pay Davies like Dixon and Allen.)

The tribunal set the fee at £90,000, which Fulham described as "an insult to the player and to us," but Davies was gone.

But not for long. His stay at Chelsea was brief, and after a short spell at Manchester City he was back at Fulham in 1986. He broke the club scoring record in 1989 and then, after a couple more seasons, moved on to Wrexham.

According to Roger Brown, Davies was "probably the laziest centre-forward there was, but Ivor was always in the right place at the right time". Ray Lewington noted that "You very rarely play with natural goalscorers like our Ivor. He was one of the very best I played with. He was an instinctive player, and his goals got us out of trouble on many occasions."

A hat-trick against Chelsea, October 1983.

On his way to scoring four against Manchester City in March 1984.

FOOTBALL -STATS-

Gordon Davies

Name: Gordon Davies

Born: Merthyr Tydfil 1955

Position: Centre-forward

Fulham playing career: 1977–1991 (elsewhere 1984–1986)

Club appearances: 450

Goals: 178

Wales appearances: 16

Goals: 2

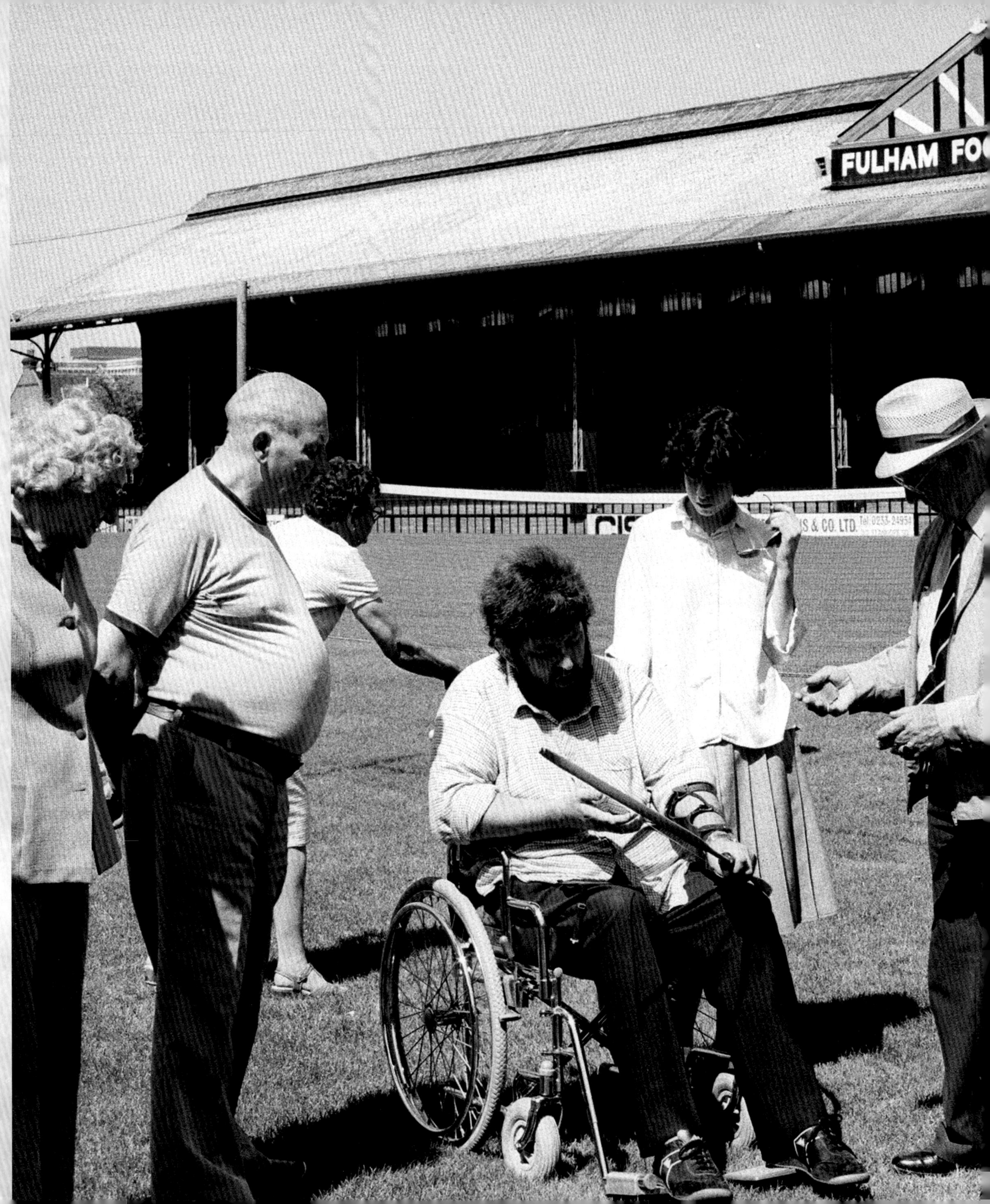
FULHAM